Navigating the World of Multimedia - Innovation and Applications

Edited by Dragan Cvetković and Yves Philippe Rybarczyk

Published in London, United Kingdom

Navigating the World of Multimedia - Innovation and Applications
http://dx.doi.org/10.5772/intechopen.1004665
Edited by Dragan Cvetković and Yves Philippe Rybarczyk

Contributors
Arwa Mashat, Dragan Cvetković, Josue Segura Montero, Marie-Laure Cazin, Mati Mõttus, Mohammadreza Forghani, Nguyen Duc Son, Pia Tikka, Sharifeh S. Mirkhalaf, Yaghoub Saberi

First published in London, United Kingdom, 2025 by IntechOpen
IntechOpen is the global imprint of INTECHOPEN LIMITED, registered in England and Wales, registration number: 11086078, 167-169 Great Portland Street, London, W1W 5PF, United Kingdom

For EU product safety concerns: IN TECH d.o.o., Prolaz Marije Krucifikse Kozulić 3, 51000 Rijeka, Croatia, info@intechopen.com or visit our website at intechopen.com.

British Library Cataloguing-in-Publication Data
A catalogue record for this book is available from the British Library

Navigating the World of Multimedia - Innovation and Applications
Edited by Dragan Cvetković and Yves Philippe Rybarczyk
p. cm.
Print ISBN 978-1-83634-293-9
Online ISBN 978-1-83634-292-2
eBook (PDF) ISBN 978-1-83634-294-6

If disposing of this product, please recycle the paper responsibly.

Meet the editors

Dragan Cvetković graduated in Aeronautics from the Faculty of Mechanical Engineering, University of Belgrade, in 1988. In the Aeronautical Department, he defended his doctoral dissertation in December 1997. So far, he has published 65 books, scripts, and practicums on computers and computer programs, aviation weapons, and flight mechanics. He has published a large number of scientific papers in the country and abroad as well. Since 20th March 2007, he has worked as an assistant professor at the SINGIDUNUM UNIVERSITY in Belgrade. He became a Full Professor in Informatics and Computing in March 2014.

Yves Rybarczyk holds a Ph.D. in Robotics from the University of Evry, France. His teaching and research activities focus on human-machine interaction. He was an assistant professor at the Nova University of Lisbon from 2007 to 2015. Subsequently, he relocated to Ecuador, where he was an Associate Professor and Head of the Intelligent & Interactive Systems Lab at Universidad de Las Américas until 2019. Currently, he is a Full Professor of Artificial Intelligence at Dalarna University in Sweden. He has participated in various projects related to the modeling and development of interactive systems. In addition to his scientific publications and editorial work, Prof. Rybarczyk's contributions are recognized as pioneering research in developing machine learning algorithms for predicting complex behaviors.

Contents

Preface

Multimedia has become an essential part of everyday life for nearly everyone. Multimedia projects and information technologies have significantly influenced how vital information is conveyed to users, transforming how information is received and processed, particularly among younger generations. This demographic is often referred to in literature as the "digital age children."

Multimedia is a broad term that refers to any media that can combine multiple types of individual mediums to create a cohesive experience. In everyday language, multimedia often describes an interactive computer project that uses text, sound, video recordings, animated elements, and film.

The introductory chapter provides an overview of modern multimedia systems and interactive media. It covers essential topics such as conceptual design, new media, human-computer interaction, graphical user interfaces, digital culture, interactive design, interactivity design, and virtual and augmented reality. A key interactivity characteristic is the dynamic interaction between humans and machines, where both parties have active and predefined roles.

The field of user experience (UX) is growing and evolving rapidly. There is a demand in the specialized scientific literature for developing high-quality products that provide better experiences for end-users. The second chapter outlines a methodology that consists of integrated stages designed to enhance UX design capabilities.

In the context of globalization, interactive products must be designed to reflect different communities' unique cultural and social characteristics. The significance of cultural identity in influencing design styles within interactive user interfaces is clear. The third chapter delves into insights from culture, psychology, and aesthetics that can enhance the design process. This approach paves the way for user experiences that are culturally adapted and relevant across digital platforms around the world.

Eye-tracking technology has been utilized across various fields for some time to measure eye movements, evaluate cognitive load, and analyze user preferences in order to adapt human-interaction systems. The fourth chapter illustrates the growing application of this technology in educational research, focusing on visual attention and interaction during learning. It also connects these findings with other physiological, perceptual, and cognitive measures.

The fifth chapter discusses the experiences of participants, often assessed through standardized scales that facilitate comparisons of relevant attitudes, emotions, and other subjective experiences among individuals. Additionally, psychophysiological metrics allow researchers to observe bodily responses indicating subconscious decision-making, arousal, or excitement.

Today, video compression and media optimization are essential for efficiently managing and transmitting multimedia data. The sixth chapter offers a thorough analysis of different video compression techniques, aiming to identify and compare these methods based on their efficiency and effectiveness.

I would like to express my sincere gratitude to all the authors and coauthors for their contribution. The successful completion of the book Navigating the World of Multimedia – Innovation and Applications resulted from the cooperation of many people. I would especially like to thank the Publishing Process Manager, Ms. Valentina Jolić, for her support during the publishing process.

Dragan Cvetković
Singidunum University,
Belgrade, Republic of Serbia

Yves Philippe Rybarczyk
Dalarna University,
Falun, Sweden

Chapter 1

Introductory Chapter: Multimedia – Innovation and Applications

Dragan Cvetković

1. Introduction

In the digital age, where visual displays, sounds, and interactive experiences merge, the role of multimedia designers has become increasingly significant—arguably more important than ever. For those who find joy in creating compelling experiences through the combination of graphics, sound, and interactive elements, a multimedia project can represent a pathway to a creative and dynamic career. It is essential to recognize that creativity has no boundaries.

Multimedia refers to the integration of various content forms, such as text, audio, images, video, and interactive elements, into a single digital platform or application. This integration creates a more engaging experience compared to traditional media that relies on a single medium.

In today's world, text and the ability to read serve as the "gateway" to knowledge and, ultimately, power. Reading and writing are vital skills in most modern societies. Throughout history, text continues to convey information that can carry powerful meanings. Following the "explosion" of the internet, the importance of text has only intensified [1].

The content displayed on a multimedia computer screen at any given moment includes a mix of text, symbols, photographic images, vector graphics, 3D representations, interactive buttons, and moving video windows. Some elements of the display can move or change position, ensuring that the screen never appears static and constantly engages the viewer's attention. The computer screen serves as an active medium; it conveys more than just a simple message; it is the essential connection between the viewer and all the content of a project [1, 2].

2. Basic elements

Sound is probably one of the most exciting components of multimedia. It serves as a universal language, understood regardless of the spoken language. Sound enriches our experiences through music, can astonish us with sensational special effects, and can influence our mood in subtle ways as background audio. The effective use of sound can be the distinguishing factor between an ordinary multimedia presentation and a truly professional, spectacular one [1].

Animation refers to the process of creating the illusion of movement using drawings, models, or inanimate objects. This effect is achieved through an optical illusion of motion based on a phenomenon known as persistence of vision. Animation can be executed in various ways. Moving video is a multimedia element that can captivate a student's attention while learning on computers. Among multimedia options, digital video is the most engaging; it serves as a powerful tool that connects computer users to the real world [1–4].

The continuous advancement of computers and information technologies enables the development and application of new methods and systems that were previously unattainable. One notable advancement is virtual reality technology, which allows the creation of virtual environments. By using virtual reality techniques, realistic simulations can be developed, offering valuable applications across many areas of human activity. While simulations have existed for some time, virtual reality can create a sense of "immersion" in a non-existent or illusory world.

3. Creating a multimedia project

Before beginning work on a multimedia project, authors must first understand the project's scope and content. They should form a clear mental image of the methods and resources available to effectively convey the desired messages to potential users. Following this, they should create a structured outline and plan that takes into account essential factors such as skills, time, budget, tools, and available resources. Proper planning is just as critical as organizing the project schedule and content.

The processes of designing and producing multimedia projects are closely interconnected. The best outcomes often arise when feedback is considered and modifications are made during production. Conversely, projects where the design phase is completed too early may reveal flaws, limiting their potential for improvement. Caution is essential, as excessive feedback and numerous changes can jeopardize a project, leading to unnecessary waste of time and money. It is important to suggest balanced changes that align with the anticipated budget [1].

Multimedia projects frequently necessitate collaboration among designers, animators, video experts, and various types of programmers. This collaborative environment fosters teamwork, preparing participants to work efficiently in interdisciplinary teams while combining diverse skill sets to create cohesive and impactful projects [5, 6].

4. Application of multimedia

Multimedia is utilized across various fields, including but not limited to advertising, art, education, entertainment, communication, engineering, medicine, mathematics, business, scientific research, and spatiotemporal applications. Here are a few examples.

In the creative industries, multimedia serves numerous purposes, ranging from fine art and entertainment to commercial art and journalism, as well as media and software services. It's important to note that multimedia designers can work across a wide array of fields throughout their careers. The demand for their skills varies from technical and analytical to creative. Additionally, the incorporation of interactivity in multimedia is particularly noteworthy, as it forms the foundation for most creative endeavors across different platforms.

Marketing and commercial practices are increasingly relying on interactive multimedia, utilizing more sophisticated techniques to enhance user engagement and attention retention. Advertising companies are turning to social media, online platforms, and television for product promotion. These channels allow businesses to specifically target their desired audience with tailored messages, advertisements, and promotions. Moreover, internal and external office communications encompass a range of materials, from engaging presentations to training sessions for new employees. By researching and analyzing data from multimedia platforms, advertisers can adapt their marketing strategies to quickly and effectively understand the demographics of their target audience. A classic example of this approach is the use of digital billboards, which can display clips from various angles to create a 3D optical illusion that captures the observer's attention. This technique takes advantage of the well-known limitations of human vision, making it a powerful tool in advertising [1].

Multimedia projects are extensively used in the entertainment industry to create special effects in films and animations, both 2D and 3D. Multimedia games and simulations have gained popularity as forms of entertainment, with a wide range of software programs available to support them. Video games and computer simulations are classified as multimedia because they combine animation, sound, and interactivity to provide players or participants with an immersive experience. While the animation styles and sound types may vary in video games, the interactive component makes them standout examples of interactive multimedia and successful projects. Interactive multimedia refers to applications that enable users to actively engage with the events within a game or simulation rather than merely observing. In the realm of the arts, some multimedia artists blend various techniques using different media that involve interaction with the viewer. For instance, they might create virtual environments of museums or art galleries, allowing users to navigate these spaces with a certain degree of freedom.

In education at all levels, multimedia is utilized to develop computer-based training courses (commonly referred to as Computer-Based Training, or CBT) and reference materials like encyclopedias and dictionaries. CBT enables users to navigate through a series of presentations, read text on specific topics, and view illustrations in various formats. It is important to note that recent advancements in multimedia have significantly expanded the theory of learning. This has led to the emergence of new research areas, including cognitive load and multimedia learning.

Multimedia provides students with alternative ways to acquire knowledge through educational technology, which is designed to enhance teaching and learning using various media and platforms. This technology allows students to learn at their own pace and enables professors to observe and respond to each student's individual needs. Lessons can be tailored to specific subjects and personalized for students with different levels of understanding of a given topic. The effective use of modern multimedia fosters interactive communication between students and professors, creating channels for feedback and promoting an active learning process that relies on new and social media. When used appropriately and not excessively, this technology can be highly beneficial for the learning experience.

In education, video games can be beneficial when used appropriately. It is particularly important to highlight that fast-paced action games play a significant role in enhancing cognitive abilities such as attention, task switching, and the ability to resist various distractions. While video games may consume some time that could be spent on school tasks, they are more likely to help redirect student attention from gaming to curricular objectives.

The global spread and development of the English language have made multimedia an essential tool for communication among diverse people and cultures. This relevance extends beyond English, as multimedia technology offers a platform for learning various languages. Research has demonstrated that multimedia motivates students to learn additional languages by providing support through audio, visuals, and animations.

The use of multimedia in journalism is increasingly apparent. News organizations worldwide are striving to adapt to this new trend by integrating multimedia practices into their operations. In some regions, this transition is occurring more slowly, while in others, it is happening more rapidly, which is to be expected. To keep pace with the evolving multimedia landscape, journalists are incorporating various multimedia elements, such as visual displays, into their reports.

Software engineers can utilize multimedia in computer simulations for a variety of purposes, ranging from entertainment to training, including industrial and military training. This area is sometimes referred to as multimedia engineering. Multimedia components with software interfaces are often created through collaboration between creative professionals and software engineers. The use of multimedia enhances teaching practices in engineering, allowing for more innovative approaches to educating future engineers and expanding their understanding of the field.

In mathematical and scientific research, multimedia is primarily utilized for modeling and simulations. This approach allows researchers to test relevant theories, verify field results, and assess whether the data is coherent. It also helps determine whether further research should progress in that direction or if adjustments are necessary. Such multimedia presentations enhance and expedite the scientific research process across nearly all fields.

Medical professors and students have numerous opportunities to learn new techniques and procedures through interactive media, online courses, and lectures. As the use of computers and technology increases, the medical field has started to adopt new devices and methods to teach students, perform procedures, and analyze patient data. This approach also helps present information in a meaningful way to patients. Additionally, the development of 3D simulators allows for complex surgeries to be practiced in a virtual environment, effectively preparing surgeons for challenging surgical procedures.

Virtual Reality (VR) is a technology that creates a simulated environment, typically through computer-generated images or a combination of real and virtual content. The aim of virtual reality is to make users feel as if they are physically present in another environment, even though they are actually located in the real world. Virtual reality has a wide range of applications, including gaming, simulations, education, healthcare, training, and entertainment.

In addition to virtual reality, it's important to mention augmented reality, which overlays digital content onto the real world using various media, such as audio, animation, and text. Augmented reality gained significant popularity in the twenty-first century.

Author details

Dragan Cvetković
Singidunum University, Belgrade, Republic of Serbia

*Address all correspondence to: dcvetkovic@singidunum.ac.rs

References

[1] Cvetković D, Savanović N. Web Design and Multimedia Systems. Belgrade, Serbia: Singidunum University; 2023

[2] Costello V. Multimedia Foundations: Core Concepts for Digital Design. 2nd ed. England: Routledge; 2016

[3] Steane J, Yee J. Interaction Design – From Concept to Completion. New York, USA: Bloomsbury Visual Arts; 2018

[4] Block B. The Visual Story: Creating the Visual Structure of Film, TV, and Digital Media. 3rd ed. England: Routledge; 2020

[5] Swarnkar SK, Annu Sharma J, Somasekar BB. Machine Learning in Multimedia: Unlocking the Power of Visual and Auditory Intelligence. 1st ed. USA: CRC Press; 2024

[6] Kukreja V, Singh A, Kaur D, Bajwa JK. Digital Cultural Heritage (Innovations in Multimedia, Virtual Reality and Augmentation). 1st ed. USA: CRC Press; 2024

Chapter 2

Development of the Skill to Design User Experience: A Case Study from the Informatics Engineering Course at the University of Matanzas

Josue Segura Montero

Abstract

The field of user experience (UX) is growing and evolving rapidly. The Cuban software industry currently demands the development of higher-into quality products that provide a better experience to end users. The specialized scientific literature states that the user experience design (UX) should be integrated into the software development processes; however, in the Cuban academic environment, the study plans and programs do not include contents that encourage the appropriation of knowledge and development of the ability to design user experience (UX) in the computer professional. A methodology was developed consisting of stages integrated as a system to develop the ability to design the user experience (UX). For this purpose, the course "Methodology of User Experience Design," located in a Virtual Learning Environment (EVA) of the Informatics Engineering course at the University of Matanzas, which allowed students to systematize actions and operations and consequently develop the ability, was used. To achieve the objective, theoretical and empirical methods of educational research were used. The Delphy method obtained the opinions and criteria of 16 experts, who theoretically validated the proposal.

Keywords: skill, user experience design, informatics engineering, methodology, the teaching of computer science, development

1. Introduction

Currently, the development and use of Information Technologies is increasingly diverse and widespread, growing at an accelerated pace and reaching significant levels. It has led to the proliferation of various software projects aimed at digitally transforming society, thereby simplifying the everyday tasks of citizens. The effective, efficient, and highly satisfying performance of these tasks is closely related to usability, which has been address by different authors from different angles and approaches [1–4].

In the current technological context, there is a high demand for usability by end users. Likewise, there is a growing interest from the software engineering community to focus systematically on the adoption of methods and practices that generate products with higher levels of usability in their development [4].

Madruga and Viltres [2] consider that usability evaluation has different perceptions, from the developer, the customer, and the end user. The latter will determine the success of the product based on their satisfaction, influenced by the usability of the product; hence, the importance of creating usable software. It is not enough to create software for a specific purpose, and it must reflect the conditions and needs of the end users who will use it to ensure its success.

Bevan [1] highlights the difference between usability and UX in terms of performance and pleasure. Each respond to the following objectives: usability, evaluation effectiveness, satisfaction, and efficiency. Build an interface that is easy to use, improve learning (UX), understand the user, what he/she does and what he/she wants, recognize, and suggest responses related to emotions.

According to Rocca [4], UX is about technology that satisfies more than instrumental needs in a way that recognizes its use as a subjective, situated, complex, and dynamic encounter. To achieve a good user experience of their products, companies must establish processes and teams responsible for user experience design.

Aveleira and Silva [5] consider that design (UX) goes beyond the pursuit of ease of use in products to achieve innovative proposals focused on creating unique experiences. It is not a closed and defined discipline but rather an open and multidisciplinary approach to work. The projections should be focused on users experiencing pleasure when interacting with the systems, framed in that the functional criteria (which are obvious) are not enough, so you must achieve an emotional dimension of use and enjoyment of an interactive application, through an emotional design approach.

In software startups, UX practices are integrated throughout the development phases, but challenges persist due to resource constraints [6]. The integration of UX techniques with business process modeling is emerging as a promising approach to improve software design, including product lifecycle management systems [7]. These studies collectively emphasize the growing importance of UX skills in software development and the need for further research to optimize UX integration in various software development environments.

Among the authors who have defined the term skills, from a psycho-pedagogical perspective [6–10], these authors, attached to the historical-cultural approach of [11], assume, in one way or another, skill as a system of actions and operations that developed in an individual, within the framework of activity, on the basis of acquired knowledge and intellectual capacities.

Ginoris et al. [8] consider skill as a component of the teaching content as it is the conscious and successful mastery of the activity. We agree with [8], when they state that the functional invariants constitute a methodological theoretical term that allows the study with greater objectivity of the execution of the action, emphasizing that its pedagogical implication lies in the fact that it is possible to achieve mastery of the same as a skill, if the systematization of the functional invariants of the execution is achieved.

In this sense, the author of the present research considers that the skill is the result of the systematization and appropriation of a set of actions and operations on the internal plane. The didactic importance of its knowledge lies in the fact that, if the conscious systematization of functional invariants as a system of execution (actions and operations) is achieved, it can be mastered as a skill.

Colin et al. [12] argue that a set of skills have not been explored in the context of UX beyond a preliminary set of digital design skills created for an educational context, focusing on a symbiosis of technical skill and communication ability [13], refers that good UX design is gaining importance within the industry when developing new products, implies that user experience (UX) design skills must be available in the development process.

According to Øvad and Larsen [14], good UX design is gaining importance within the industry when developing new software products and implies that user experience (UX) design skills must be available in the development process. The field of user experience (UX) is growing and evolving rapidly, as instructors who teach and help design (UX) programs for higher education students.

Recent research highlights the changing role of user experience (UX) in software development. UX designers require visual interface design skills, while UX researchers need proficiency in usability studies and interviews [15].

User experience (UX) design methodologies have evolved to address the increasing complexity of digital products and user needs. Traditional approaches include interaction design and user experience design, while newer methodologies such as Agile, Lean (UX), and Design Sprint have emerged from commercial perspectives [13].

Research on user experience (UX) design methodologies in university environments reveals several approaches. Agile methodologies combined with user-centered design have been proposed for identifying usability issues in the early stages of educational software development [16].

According to Riascos and Estrada [17], universities play a significant role in the software industry insofar as they are the educators of professionals in the IT field. Consequently, higher education institutions (HEIs) offer academic programs related to systems engineering, software engineering, and computer engineering; however, in many cases, these programs do not include courses related to user experience design (UX).

Training software developers in simplified (UX) methods through on-site hands-on sessions have shown promise in integrating (UX) considerations into agile industrial environments [14]. Teaching (UX) design to IT students presents challenges due to its interdisciplinary nature, requiring educators to foster creativity and customer-driven thinking [15]. These methodologies aim to bridge the gap between academic research and practical application, emphasizing the need of adapting methods (UX) to fit diverse developmental contexts and educational needs.

According to Barroso BenÃ\-tez et al. [18], taking user experience (UX) into account in the framework of industrial development offers transparency, inspection, and adaptation. Its application is recommended from the early stages of development, as well as the training of personnel involved in the matter. In this way, design, evaluation, and control styles available in agile paradigms are taken advantage of.

Cuervo [19] considers that the UX has matured in recent years and has evolved as a competitive factor in the development of software products and services in Cuba; however, difficulties have been detected in the Cuban academic environment, due to the insufficient approach to the reality of the conditions of the software industry. The Cuban software industry is mainly focused on functionality issues. The steps toward usability and UX are still relatively slow, and there is no mention of aspects that allow the analysis of UX nor the inclusion of UX in the measurements [18].

Segura [20] suggests the need to expand the topics that include the end-user experience (UX) when interacting with the software as a guarantee of product quality, ensuring from the university curriculum the preparation of more competent professionals in this area of scientific knowledge. There is a need to deepen these aspects where the end-user experience when interacting with the software is taken into account, among other issues, as a guarantee of product quality.

Currently, the design of the curriculum of the career of computer engineering in Cuba, which is based on the experience gained in the realization of economic and social transformations that occurred in the country, has a strong emphasis, among other issues, on developing skills in the computer professional, so that it allows to develop quality software, according to international trends in software development. Among the disciplines of the career that enable this purpose is the discipline of software engineering and management, which among its general objectives, proposes to develop software management processes, ensuring the quality of software products [21].

Due to the vertiginous development of computer science and the objectives of this discipline, it is difficult to define the subjects that conform to the curriculum. In this sense, the study plans to raise some subjects that constitute important proposals, among which software quality stands out. The University of Matanzas is part of the network of Higher Education Centers of Cuba (CES), where the Informatics Engineering degree is taught in the daytime and blended modalities.

During the development of the teaching-learning process of the degree, the optional subject "Usability in Software Development (USD)" is developed, which addresses the essential elements to evaluate the usability of a computer product, however, design contents (UX) are not addressed in the subject, therefore the skill of designing the user experience (UX) that contributes to the training of more competent professionals according to the demands of society is not developed.

From the above considerations, it could be established as a fundamental contradiction of this investigation between the need to enhance the contents of user experience design (UX) during the software development process and the insufficient theoretical and methodological treatment given to the ability to design user experience (UX) in the Computer Engineering career at the University of Matanzas. A descriptive exploratory study was conducted to determine the theoretical and methodological treatment given to the ability to design user experience during the software development process in the career, and the following question was asked.

How to develop the skill to design user experience in the Computer Engineering career at the University of Matanzas?

2. Methods

To determine how to develop the skill to design user experience in the Computer Engineering career at the University of Matanzas, different methods were used at the theoretical and empirical level. In this sense, the historical-logical method allowed studying the treatment given to the ability to design the user experience (UX) during the software development process, particularly in the Computer Engineering career at the University of Matanzas. The analytical-synthetic method made it possible to break down the essential concepts of the skill for the analysis of its particularities, and, with these elements, it is possible to use the definitions and general characteristics of the skill of designing user experience as a synthesis.

The Study Plan E which governs the Computer Engineering career at the University of Matanzas was consulted, as well as the study plan of the Software Engineering and Management discipline, the methodological orientations offered there and the didactic treatment given to the contents of user experience design, in the subject

Usability in Software Development taught in the career, which together with the consultation and theoretical systematization of national and international literature, related to the subject of study, allowed establishing the regularities on the internal structure and functional invariants of the ability to design the user experience (UX), during the software development process in the Informatics Engineering course at the University of Matanzas.

Interviews were conducted with students of the regular daytime course belonging to the fourth year of the 22nd and 23rd academic years, who receive the subject Usability in Software Development, where it was possible to verify the lack of knowledge on the subject, in that sense most of the students in their answers associated it to software usability or reduced it only to the metrics that characterize the evaluation of usability of a computer product, but they failed to provide many more elements. We reviewed the graduation degree works corresponding to the 21st, 22nd, and 23rd academic years, showing a reduced number of degree work elements related to the user experience (UX) and the need to take it into account during the development of their computer systems.

Interviews were conducted with 13 teachers who taught different subjects in their careers, in order to verify the knowledge they had on the subject, and criteria were obtained on the treatment they give to the development of the ability to design the user experience (UX). In this sense, they do not expose students to the importance and purpose of the ability to design the user experience (UX) as they do not know its internal structure and have little mastery of it, as can be seen in the results of **Figure 1**.

The above results highlight the need to find ways, forms, methods, and procedures that contribute to the development of the skill of designing user experience (UX). Therefore, the author concludes the need to develop a methodology to solve this difficulty. The Delphy method was used to obtain the opinions and criteria of 16 experts, which allowed obtaining a general consensus, which allowed the theoretical validation of the proposed methodology.

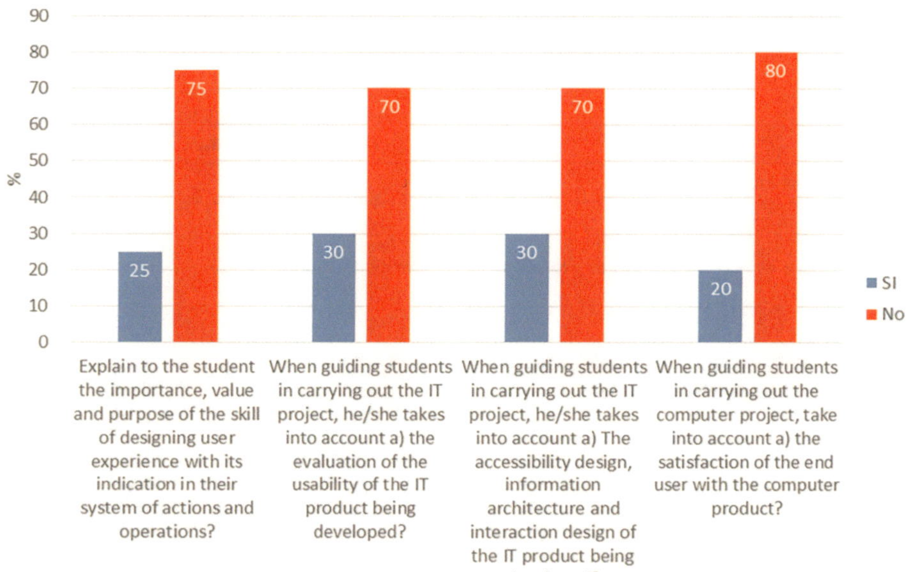

Figure 1.
Results of the survey with the teachers who teach different subjects in the degree.

3. Results and discussion

Based on the systematization made on the subject under study by several authors of [1, 11, 12, 15, 18, 22–24]. From a psycho-pedagogical and computer science point of view, the author defines the ability to design the user experience (UX) in the context of the Computer Engineering Career at the University of Matanzas as the system of actions and operations that students develop during the development activity of the computer product in its life cycle, which takes into account the sensation, feeling, emotional response, evaluation, and satisfaction of the end user.

To achieve this purpose, in the opinion of the author of this research, the conscious systematization of the functional invariants (actions and operations) of the skill to design the user experience (UX) is required. To achieve this purpose, the conscious systematization of the functional invariants of the skill of designing user experience (UX) is required (**Tables 1–5**).

1. Action: Evaluate the usability of the computer product	Operations
	• Determine the efficiency of the computer product. • Determine the effectiveness of the computer product. • Determine the recognition of the computer product. • Determine the ease of learning the computer product. • Determine the protection against errors of the computer product. • Determine the esthetics of the user interface, of the computer product.

Source: Own elaboration.

Table 1.
Action: Evaluate the usability of the computer product with its corresponding operations.

2. Action: Design an accessible computing product.	Operations
	• Develop a perceivable computer product. • Develop a workable computer product. • Develop an understandable computer product. • Develop a robust software product.

Source: Own elaboration.

Table 2.
The action: Design an accessible software product with its corresponding operations.

3. Action: Determine the information architecture of the computer product.	Operations
	• Identify user needs. • Organize computer product information. • Classify computer product information. • Structure the information of the computer product. • Define the labels and labels of the computer product. • Evaluate the information architecture of the computer product.

Source: Own elaboration.

Table 3.
The action: Determine the information architecture of the software product with its corresponding operations.

DOI: http://dx.doi.org/10.5772/intechopen.1006928

4. Action: Design IT Product Interaction	Operations
	• Analyze and evaluate user needs. • Define the behavior that the interface will have in the interaction with the users. • Design prototypes of the computer product • Use evaluation methods of the user centered design.

Table 4.
The action: Design IT Product Interaction with its corresponding operations.

5. Action: Determine user satisfaction with the computer product	Operations
	• Carry out interviews and surveys of users (to determine the behavior, attitude, feelings, and emotions of users about aspects of the computer product) • Carry out moderate tests (to check the completion by users of the tasks of the computer product) • Carry out beta tests (for several users on a platform in the final stages of the development of the software product) • Perform A/B tests (to measure the effectiveness of a specific design that guides the user to perform a specific action)
Source: Own elaboration.	

Table 5.
The action: Determine the user's satisfaction with the computer product with its corresponding operations.

4. General objective of the methodology

To structure a system of procedures that contribute to the development of the skill to design the user experience (UX) during the software development process in the Informatics Engineering course at the University of Matanzas.

5. Methodology structure

The methodology has a general objective and two components, one theoretical and one instrumental, which are structured in three stages: diagnosis of the prerequisites of the subject (first stage), the introduction of information and communication technologies (ICT) for the preparation of the subject (second stage), and integration of the problem-based approach with the project approach during software development in the Computer Engineering course at the University of Matanzas, the structure of which can be seen in **Figure 2**.

The stages of the methodology are interrelated and logically arranged systemically. A relationship of subordination is established between the stages, diagnosis of the prerequisites of the subject, and introduction of ICT for the preparation of the subject, in which the necessary conditions are created for the subsequent development of the user experience (UX) design skill, which occurs in the stage of integration of the problem statement and the problem statement. In this stage, the fundamental actions and procedures for the development of the user experience (UX) design skill are

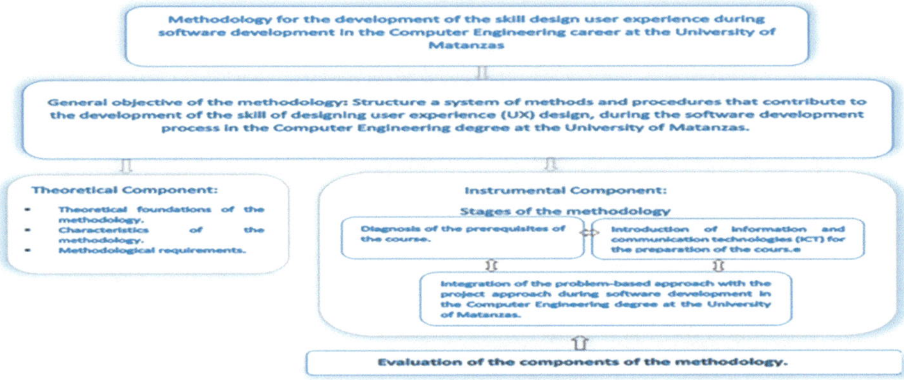

Figure 2.
Structure of the methodology.

developed, which correspond to the different stages of the software development life cycle: analysis, design, implementation, and validation. In this sense, during the solution of the software project, students rely on user experience design knowledge to solve subproblems. To do so, they perform a set of actions and operations that allow them to integrate into the software development phases, thus contributing to the development of user experience (UX) design competence.

The following is a brief description of the procedures for each stage and their contribution to the development of user experience (UX) design skills.

Stage 1: Diagnosis of the preconditions of the subject. The objective of the stage is to diagnose the level of assurance of the conditions present before the development of the user experience (UX) design skill in the subject and, based on this, to take the pertinent measures for its assurance.

Stage 2: Introduction of IT for the preparation of the subject. The objective of this stage is to introduce IT as a support for the subject and to systematize the knowledge acquired in the different stages of development of the IT project to develop in the students the skills to design the user experience (UX). It is addressed to each student using the course "User Experience (UX) Design Methodology," available in the institutional repository of the University of Matanzas (https://eva.umcc.cu). The topics conceived in the course can be seen in the **Figure 3**.

For this purpose, it is supported by the didactic material available on the platform., https://eva.umcc.cu which is used by the students during the different stages of the development of the IT project, and in this way, they develop the skills to design the user experience.

Procedures:

Develop the user experience (UX) design methodology course on the platform https://eva.umcc.cu.

- Locate on the platform the available resources of the course, which contribute to systematizing the actions and operations of user experience design that facilitate the development of the user experience design (UX) competence.

- Create forums in the course available on the platform, for the discussion of aspects related to the learning activities, to acquire new knowledge through

Figure 3.
User experience (UX) design methodology course topics (https://eva.umcc.cu).

debate. In this way, knowledge is built collectively from the answers to the questions asked by the students, encouraging reflection and criticism based on the problems presented by them, during the implementation of the IT project to correspond to their motivations and future aspirations.

Stage 3: Integration of the problem-based approach with the project approach during the teaching-learning process in the Computer Engineering course at the University of Matanzas.

- The objective of this stage is to integrate the computer projects carried out by the students in the subject with the contents located in the course available on the platform https://eva.umcc.cu so that they promote the solution of problems that contribute both to the training and to the development of the ability to design the user experience (UX). For this purpose, the problem-based approach is introduced and integrated into the project approach throughout the different stages of the software development life cycle.

At this stage, the software project enables the integration of the problem-based approach with the project approach while ensuring the necessary problematic for the solution of the subproblems. In the solution of the subproblems of the software development life cycle: analysis, design, implementation, and validation, the students deploy the actions and operations necessary to develop the competency that subsequently validates if it meets the requirements of the software product to be developed and if can be used to solve other problems.

Procedures.

- The teacher guides the solution of the computer project during which the student faces different types of didactic problems during the teaching-learning process in a project context.

- The teacher, based on his experience, must take the teaching problems that arise from the students' practice, linked to each of their computer projects and the level of development of each of them.

- The teacher must promote spaces of exchange and cooperation for the achievement of the informatics project, as well as its development, where students have a leading role in decision-making.

- The teacher requires the student to divide the problem into subproblems, with functionality during the development of the project.

To accomplish this goal, the "User Experience (UX) Design Methodology" course, which is available on the platform https://eva.umcc.cu, has been introduced as a new supporting element. To achieve this, eight activities have been proposed to be conducted with the students to enhance their skills to design user experience (UX). Examples of some of these activities are provided in **Tables 6** and 7.

It is crucial to note that each of the proposed activities (eight) is systemic in nature and interconnected. Each activity has a distinct objective and requires specific steps that correspond to the subject matter addressed in the online course platform. This is

Activity #1. It should be done in the second week of classes, which corresponds to activity #2 of the program of the subject
This activity consists of the teacher guiding the students in the search for real problems in their environment and linking them to their computer projects, where the solution will promote learning and interaction by confronting them with diverse experiences, which will transform their learning and increase their capacity to process information, by sharing experiences with their classmates in an environment of collaboration, respect, and attention to individual differences and disinterested help, which will have an important impact on their motivations and future aspirations.
Objective of the activity: Characterize the essential elements of the IT project to be developed taking into account the user experience (UX) during the selection of each of your IT projects.
Proposal: Develop the course project.
Development: Five steps must be carried out
Step 1: Present a topic for the project.
This first step, of an introductory nature, is carried out with the whole group in the classroom, communicating the interests and scope of the computer project, the teacher, as well as the students, must make statements about the essential elements of the computer project and the expectations they have about it
Step 2: Project proposal. The first agreements on the project must be established in the course available on the platform (https://eva.umcc.cu). The necessary indications to develop it are expressed. At this point, the students must identify and specify the theme of the project to be developed by the teams created and propose the theme of each of their IT projects.
Step 3: The teacher should analyze with the students the IT projects, elaborated in other courses, and IT products elaborated by IT professionals that take into account elements of user experience design (UX). The students should establish comparisons between professional products and IT projects developed in previous courses by other students and how they can provide solutions taking into account appropriate elements of user experience design (UX)
Step 4: The teacher has to take advantage of the difficulties present in the software products developed by the students in other courses, to demonstrate why it is necessary to take into account user experience (UX) design during software development, establishing analogies with real-world problems.
Step 5: Processing and development of the IT project. Students must begin to develop their IT projects based on the problems that are generated in their solution, integrating the knowledge they receive in the course with the knowledge of user experience design (UX) with system characters that are presented in the course "Methodology of user experience design (UX)" available on the platform (https://eva.umcc.cu). The objective of the teaching task is to appropriate knowledge of user experience design (UX) with system character, in correspondence with the motivations and aspirations of the students. This teaching task must be oriented and guided by the teacher during all the development stages of the IT project.

Table 6.
Activity #1 Example of an activity to be done with students to develop the skill of designing user experience (UX).

***Activity #3.* To be done in the fourth week of classes, which corresponds to activity no. 4 of the program on the subject "Usability in Software Development"**
Objective of the activity: To evaluate the usability of the software development, by integrating the design into the user experience (UX) during the realization of the IT project.
Proposal: It is carried out in the fourth week of classes of the course Usability in Software Development. The professor oriented the study of Topic 2: The user experience and its relationship with the evaluation of usability in software products of the course available on the platform with the following teaching content: Characteristics of usability and its relationship with the user experience. The effectiveness, efficiency, recognition, ease of learning, error protection, and esthetics of the user interface of a computer product.
Development: Four steps must be carried out
Step 1: The teacher has selected the problem present in one of the projects carried out by the students and can ask the following: Problematic questions and indications, namely, how to get the user of the computer system to complete the task through the developed functionalities, what elements must be taken into account for the user of the computer system to complete the tasks in time, how to deal with possible errors that may occur when the user interacts with the computer product, and how to ensure that the user learns easily to operate the computer system?
The teacher can establish as a heuristic strategy the decomposition of functionalities of already developed computer systems in such a way that the students visualize the elements that correctly evidence the efficiency, effectiveness, protection against errors, and esthetics of the user interfaces so that as the student develops the different functionalities of his computer projects, he integrates these elements. The impulses given by the teacher allow the student aware of the functional invariants of the action to evaluate the usability of the computer product that the student is expected to master.
Step 2: Once the previous step is completed, the teacher should guide the student to rely on the study of lessons 3, 4, and 5 and perform the teaching tasks 4 and 5 corresponding to Topic 2: The User Experience and its relationship with the evaluation of usability in computer products of the course available on the platform in order to determine the effectiveness, efficiency, recognition, ease of learning, error protection, and esthetics of the user interface of a computer product
Step 3: Once the second step has been completed, the student must exchange with the other students the teaching tasks 4 and 5 corresponding to topic 2 of the course, during the realization of his/her IT project
With the help of the teacher who teaches the course, and with the other students, they should develop activities related with these contents in their computer project with a high level of confrontation and variant analysis. This step should be performed in independent study after the activity has been oriented.

Table 7.
Activity #1 Example of an activity to be done with students to develop the skill of designing user experience (UX).

intended to systematize the actions and operations and, consequently, to develop the ability to design user experience (UX).

To assess whether the methodology enables the intended objective to be met, the quality with which the actions of the initial diagnosis stages were executed to create preconditions must be checked, as well as the implementation of the procedures of each stage. To do so, it is recommended to use the following control instruments:

Stages of implementation of the actions: Initial diagnostic stage:

1. Document review guide: to determine whether all necessary and sufficient documents for this stage were reviewed and to what extent these were useful for the next stage.

2. Survey questionnaire for teachers: to check to what extent they are prepared in theoretical-methodological aspects, which are required for the implementation of the methodology

3. Verification of the quality of the program of the subject "Usability in Software" [20] (https://eva.umcc.cu).

To evaluate the proposal before its implementation in educational practice, sixteen experts evaluated the application of the Delphy Method [21]. For this purpose, they were offered different elements so that they could offer their criteria on the methodology, namely, (1) theoretical, psychological, pedagogical, and didactic foundations; (2) general bases of the methodology; (3) graphic representation of the methodology; (4) general objective of the methodology; (5) stages of the methodology; (6) methodological actions; (7) procedures.

A sequence of steps is executed to allow its application. For this purpose, the following steps were executed: elaboration of the objective; selection of the experts; choice of the methodology; execution of the selected methodology; and the processing of the information. The experts self-evaluate themselves through a questionnaire to be selected.

The competence of each expert is determined by the Competence Coefficient (K). The coefficient of knowledge or information that the expert possesses about the problem (based on his self-assessment) is represented in equation by the term Kc, and the coefficient of argumentation or substantiation of the expert's criteria is denoted by the term Ka [25].

$$K = (Kc + Ka))/2 \tag{1}$$

Each expert is selected if the competence coefficient is in the range $0.8 \leq K \leq 1$, as shown in the figure. In the research, the experts who met this condition were selected 16 experts which can be seen in **Table 8**. The experts were asked to evaluate the didactic strategy by assigning a quantitative value [1–10], decreasing according to their estimation on the requested scale. In addition, they were asked to explain the weaknesses and strengths that, in their opinion, could be present in the proposed didactic strategy, as well as other relevant aspects not contemplated and which, in their opinion, should be present (**Table 9**).

The argumentation coefficient Ka is calculated by means of the following equation:

$$Ka = \sum ni = (n1 + n2 + n3 + n3 + n4 + n5 + n6) \tag{2}$$

Sources that have influenced your knowledge on the subject	Degree of influence of each of the sources		
	High	Medium	Low
Theoretical analysis performed	0.30	0.20	0.10
His experience in teaching and research practice at the higher education level.	0.50	0.40	0.20
Consultation of research in design (UX) by Cuban or foreign authors.	0.05	0.05	0.05
Knowledge acquired by master's or doctorate degree	0.05	0.05	0.05
Knowledge about design (UX) and its relationship with other disciplines.	0.05	0.05	0.05
Your intuition based on your professional knowledge and experience	0.05	0.05	0.05

Table 8.
Calculation of the competence coefficient Ka.

	Ka	Kc	K
E1	0.95	0.9	0.925
E2	0.7	0.9	0.8
E3	0.85	0.90	0.88
E4	0.8	0.90	0.85
E5	0.9	0.80	0.85
E6	0.8	0.80	0.80
E7	0.9	0.80	0.85
E8	0.7	0.90	0.80
E9	0.8	0.90	0.85
E10	0.7	0.90	0.80
E11	0.8	0.90	0.85
E12	0.8	0.90	0.85
E13	0.9	0.90	0.90
E14	0.9	0.70	0.80
E15	0.9	0.80	0.85
E16	0.7	0.90	0.80

Table 9.
Results of the coefficient of competence to select the experts.

The results of the competence coefficient for each expert are analyzed as follows:
$0.8 \leq K \leq 1.0$, high competence coefficient.
$0.5 \leq K < 0.8$, medium competence coefficient.
$K < 0.5$, low competence coefficient.
Guide to aspects valued by experts (**Table 10**).

To perform the statistical processing for the data obtained from the experts, Kendall's coefficient of concordance (W) was used. This coefficient allows the degree of agreement among the experts who evaluated the proposed methodology. The magnitude of Kendall's coefficient of concordance is in the range $0 \leq W \leq 1$. Values close to zero express disagreement in the concordance between experts and values close to one express maximum concordance. To calculate Kendall's correlation coefficient (W), the formula proposed in the work of is assumed, reflected in the equation.

$$U = \sum_{j=1}^{n} \left(\sum Rij\right)^2 \tag{3}$$

The terms of the equation denote m number of experts; n number of aspects to be evaluated. The term U is the quadratic summation of the Rij, expressed in equation. The sum of ranks corresponds to the experts' evaluation of question j, where Rij is the rank associated with expert (i)'s evaluation of question (j).

$$Ka = \sum ni = (n1 + n2 + n3 + n3 + n4 + n5 + n6) \tag{4}$$

The values given by each of the experts to the aspects of the guide are shown in **Tables 11**, and **12** shows the range of scores linked to each other.

Mark each aspect of the guide with a value from 1 to 10, according to the level of importance you attribute to it.
__ Proficiency in HCI, user experience (UX) methodology of working (UX) in agile environments
__ Mastering UX methodology in agile environments for software development
.__ Proficiency in training and skills development (UX)
__ Proficiency in usability evaluation, accessibility, information architecture, interaction design, user-centered design, and UX evaluation methods and techniques.
__ How are the teaching activities designed, what participatory methods are used, how are the teaching methods and means used to achieve the objectives of the program?
__ Mastery of the career objectives, professional profile, modes of action and functions of the professional.
Explain the weaknesses of the methodology.
Explain the strengths of the proposed methodology
Would you like to suggest any aspect to be taken into account in the development of the methodology?

Table 10.
Guide to aspects valued by experts.

Experts (i)				**Aspects (j)**				
	A(j = 1)	**A(j = 2)**	**A(j = 3)**	**A(j = 4)**	**A(j = 5)**	**A(j = 6)**	**A(j = 7)**	**A(j = 8)**
E(i = 1)	9	10	8	8	10	8	7	9
E(i = 2)	10	9	10	10	10	10	10	10
E(i = 3)	10	9	10	10	8	10	10	7
E(i = 4)	10	9	7	8	8	7	8	7
E(i = 5)	8	10	8	8	8	9	8	10
E(i = 6)	7	8	9	9	8	10	10	10
E(i = 7)	9	8	9	9	9	9	10	10
E(i = 8)	9	8	10	9	9	9	8	10
E(i = 9)	9	10	8	8	7	8	7	7
E(i = 10)	7	7	10	8	10	10	7	8
E(i = 11)	9	10	10	8	9	8	10	8
E(i = 12)	8	9	10	9	10	9	10	8
E(i = 13)	8	10	10	8	8	8	9	9
E(i = 14)	9	9	9	10	10	9	9	10
E(i = 15)	8	8	10	8	8	8	10	8
E(i = 16)	10	8	7	10	8	8	10	7

Table 11.
Values given by each of the experts to the aspects of the guide.

The result of the calculation of the concordance coefficient indicates that there is concordance in the experts' assessment when evaluating the methodology proposal. If the value of $W > 0.5$, the coincidence of the experts' opinions is verified.

Experts (i)	Aspects (j)							
	A(j = 1)	A(j = 2)	A(j = 3)	A(j = 4)	A(j = 5)	A(j = 6)	A(j = 7)	A(j = 8)
E(i = 1)	4.5	3.5	4.33	4.33	3.5	4.33	7	4.5
E(i = 2)	4.85	9	4.85	4.85	4.85	4.85	4.85	4.85
E(i = 3)	4.2	9	4.2	4.2	8	4.2	4.2	7
E(i = 4)	10	9	5.66	5.33	5.33	5.66	5.33	5.66
E(i = 5)	4	5	4	4	4	9	4	5
E(i = 6)	7	3.5	3.5	3.5	3.5	7	7	7
E(i = 7)	3.8	8	3.8	3.8	3.8	3.8	7.5	7.5
E(i = 8)	4	4.5	5.5	4	4	4	4.5	5.5
E(i = 9)	9	10	4.3	4.3	6.66	4.3	6.66	6.66
E(i = 10)	3.33	3.33	4.66	6	4.66	4.66	3.33	6
E(i = 11)	3	4	4	6	3	6	4	6
E(i = 12)	4.5	4	5	4	5	4	5	4.5
E(i = 13)	4	2.5	2.5	4	4	4	7.5	7.5
E(i = 14)	3.8	3.8	3.8	5.6	5.6	3.8	3.8	5.6
E(i = 15)	4.3	4.3	5	4.3	4.3	4.3	5	4.3
E(i = 16)	4	4.3	5.5	4	4.3	4.3	4	5.5
$\sum Ri$	78.28	87.73	70.60	72.21	74.50	78.20	83.67	93.07
$\sum (Ri)^2$	6127.76	7696.55	4984.36	5214.28	5550.25	6115.24	7000.67	8662.02

Table 12.
Range of linked scores.

$$W = [(12 * 51351.14)\text{-}(3 * 162 * 8 * (8 + 1)2)]/[162 * 8 * (83\text{-}1)] = 0.91 \tag{5}$$

To perform this test, the significance test with Kendall's W concordance coefficient is used. For this purpose, the following null hypothesis (Ho) and alternative hypothesis (H1) are proposed: Ho: chance coincidence (there is no association between them); H1: non-chance coincidence (there is an association between them).

$$U \sum (Rij)^2 = 51351.14 \tag{6}$$

Each statistical assessment test compares the results of the typing formulas with one of the theoretical reference distributions. To know the value of Chi-square statistic (|2), the calculation is made by means of the formula of the equation, which contemplates the equivalence of (|2) for n > 7, with (n-1) degrees of freedom (df) [26].

$$\chi^2 = m(n-1)\,W \tag{7}$$

Once the statistic (|2) is calculated, it is contrasted with the critical value of the percentage theoretical distribution (|2p), which is obtained by setting the significance level (α) and the (df). The value of (χ2p) is obtained from the Chi-square theoretical distribution table [26].

$$\chi 2 = 16(8\text{-}1)\,(0.91) = 101.92;\ \text{para df} = (\text{n-1}) = 7 \qquad (8)$$

If (|2) ≤ (|2p), the null hypothesis is accepted, the variables are independent. Si (|2) > (|2p); we reject the null hypothesis, and the variables are not independent (there is an association relationship). The value of (|2p) for 7 df with a significance level α =0.01 corresponds to a value of (|2.99) =18.5.

The result of the comparison shows that (|2) > (|2.99). This allows the null hypothesis to be rejected and the alternative hypothesis to be accepted; in other words, it confirms that there is a non-coincidental coincidence between the experts.

By applying the Delphy method, the specialists who participated in the research were selected as expert evaluators of the proposed methodology. The experts' considerations made it possible to introduce changes in the stages of the methodology. The calculation of Kendall's coefficient of concordance applied to the results of the evaluation of the methodology obtained a value of 0.91, a result that allows affirming that there is a high degree of concordance among the experts.

A reliability of 99.9% is achieved, which allows arguing that there is a high degree of agreement among the 16 experts on the effectiveness of the methodology for the development of the skill under study in the context of the Computer Engineering career at the University of Matanzas. The results of the validation of the methodology confirmed its validity, by promoting consensus among experts in the conception that it is possible to develop the user experience design skill in the Computer Engineering degree at the University of Matanzas.

6. Conclusions

The exploratory descriptive study allowed an approach to the theoretical-methodological foundations that support the user experience (UX) competence during the software development process in the context of the Computer Engineering degree at the University of Matanzas.

The results of the validation of the methodology confirmed its validity, by promoting consensus among experts in the conception that it is possible to develop the user experience design skill in the Computer Engineering degree at the University of Matanzas, making it possible to be a reference in other educational contexts as long as they are adapted to them.

The teaching of User Experience (UX) must continue to be perfected in the Cuban academic environment, as its guide and concepts define a path to follow to reach parameters accepted in the international community regarding end-user satisfaction, which guarantees the preparation of more competent professionals in Computer Engineering degrees and emerges as an urgent and relevant need today.

Conflict of interest

The author declares no conflict of interest.

Author details

Josue Segura Montero
Doctor of Education, Universidad de Matanzas, Matanzas, Cuba

*Address all correspondence to: josuesemoentero@gmail.com

References

[1] Bevan N. What Is the Difference between the Purpose of Usability and User Experience Evaluation Methods. 2009. Disponible en: https://api.semanticscholar.org/CorpusID:15182858 [citado 25 de febrero de 2023]

[2] Madruga D, Viltres H. A usability evaluation of software products: A practical case study. Publishing. 2018;**14** (3):525-541

[3] Pinto J, Agredo V, Collazos C. Constructing a guide for the evaluation 14 of usability in EVAs. EVAs. 2018;**7**(2): 93-104

[4] Rocca J. Analysis of Software Processes Oriented to Usability. 2018. Disponible en: https://dspace.ort.edu.uy/handle/20.500.11968/3733 [citado 4 de marzo de 2023]

[5] Aveleira Y, Silva D. Computer user experience design laboratory. Cuban Journal of Agricultural Science. 2011;**5** (3):1-7

[6] Talizina T. Teaching Psychology. Moscow: Progress; 1988

[7] Talizina N, Quintana Y. The activity approach in psychology and its relationship with the historical-cultural approach of L. S. Vygotsky. 2010;**230**:4-8

[8] Ginoris O, Addine F, Turcaz J. General Didactic. Basic Material, Master's Degree in Education. Latin American and Caribbean Pedagogical Institute; 2006. Available from: https://scholar.google.com.cu/citations?view_op=view_citation&hl=es&user=Ivtoi_AAAAAJ&citation_for_view=Ivtoi_AAAAAJ:8k81kl-MbHgC

[9] Savin NV. Pedagogía [Internet]. La Habana: Pueblo y educación; 1972. Available from: https://opacbiblioteca.uapa.edu.do/bib/11290

[10] Petrovsky. General Psychology. Havana. Cuba: People and Education; 1986

[11] Vygotsky L. Mind in Society: The Development of Higher Psychological Processes [Internet]. Harvard University Press; 1980. 159 p. Available from: https://books.google.com.cu/books?id=Irq913lEZ1QC

[12] Colin M, Austin T, Shad G. Flow of competence in UX design practice. In: Proceedings of the 2015 CHI Conference on Human Factors in Computing Systems; Seoul, South Korea. 2015. pp. 3285-3294

[13] Wu Y. The scope and analysis of design methodologies for user experience in interaction design. En: HCI International 2023 Posters, C Stephanidis, M Antona, S Ntoa, G Salvendy, Eds, Cham: Springer Nature Switzerland. 2023. p. 169-175.

[14] Øvad T, Larsen LB. How to reduce the UX bottleneck – Train your software developers. Behaviour and Information Technology. 2016;**35**:1080-1090

[15] Wang R, Yang J, Asser L. User experience (UX) matters: What are the most desired skills in the UX designer and UX researcher job ads. Journal of Communications Technology. 2021;**4**(2): 82-105

[16] González-González CS, Toledo-Delgado P, Muñoz-Cruz V. Agile human centered methodologies to develop educational software. Dyna. 2015;**82**: 187-194

[17] Riascos C, Estrada R. Human-computer interaction in the curriculum

of higher education institutions in Colombia. Revista de Investigación, Desarrollo e Innovación. 2018;**9**(1): 147-162

[18] Barroso BenÃ\-Tez Y, Trujillo CasaÃpmola Y, Millet LY. Marco de trabajo de evaluaciÃ³n de experiencia de usuario en el desarrollo de software. Revista Cubana de Ciencias Informáticas. 2021;**15**:92-117

[19] Cuervo RR. Evaluation of the user experience in the Cuban context. Ridtec. 2019;**15**(2):27-37

[20] Segura J. The teaching of usability in software development: Case study in the computer engineering career at the University of Matanzas. International Journal of Engineering Pedagogy. 2021; **11**(1):4-15

[21] Artola Pimentel ML, Tarifa Lozano L, Finalé, de la Cruz L. Planes de estudio e en la educaciión superior cubana: una mirada desde la educaciÃ3n continua. Revista Universidad y Sociedad. 2019;**11**: 364-371

[22] Hassan Y. Experience: Principles and Method. 2015. Disponible en: https://yusef.es/Experiencia_de_Usuario.pdf [citado 15 de enero de 2022]

[23] Rose EJ, Putnam C, MacDonald CM. Preparing future UX professionals: Human skills, technical skills, and dispositions. En: Proceedings of the 38th ACM International Conference on Design of Communication. New York, NY, USA: Association for Computing Machinery; 2020. (SIGDOC '20). Disponible en: doi:10.1145/3380851.3416774

[24] Harutyunyan N, Riehle D. User Experience Design in Software Product Lines User Experience Design in Software Product. 2019. Disponible en: https://hdl.handle.net/10125/60187I [citado 14 de mayo de 2023]

[25] Reguant M, Torrado M. El mètode Delphi. Revista d'innovació i recerca en educació. 2016;**9**(1):87-102

[26] Sheskin D. Handbook-of-Parametric-and-Nonparametric-Statistical-Procedures Second Edition [Internet]. Boca Raton, London, New York, Washington, D.C: Shapman & Hall/CRC; 2000. Available from: https://pdfcoffee.com/handbook-of-parametric-and-nonparametric-statistical-procedurespdf-pdf-free.html [Accessed: 30 December 2024]

Chapter 3

Exploring User Cultural Identity in Shaping Reflective Design Style on Interactive User Interfaces

Nguyen Duc Son

Abstract

In the context of globalization, interactive products need to be designed to reflect individual cultures and social communities. The research reveals the significance of cultural identity in influencing design styles within interactive user interfaces. Understanding how diverse cultural backgrounds impact user preferences and interactions is essential for creating inclusive and effective designs. This research focuses on the intersection of cultural identity and design aesthetics, exploring how users' cultural heritage, beliefs, and values play a key role in shaping reflective design styles. By incorporating these cultural elements into interactive interface design, designers can foster connections and enhance user engagement and experience. The chapter aims to uncover insights in culture, psychology and aesthetics that enrich the design process. As a result, it paves the way for culturally responsive and resonant user experiences across digital platforms all over the world.

Keywords: aesthetic expression, cultural identity, culturally responsive, interactive user interface, reflective design

1. Introduction

1.1 Background and context

In the context of globalization today, the issue of cultural identity is always a core issue in social activities, especially in communication activities and interactions between people in society or between people and machines... In the ever-evolving field of interactive user interface (UI) design, the integration of users' cultural identity into reflective design styles is becoming increasingly important. Furthermore, human-centered design has become the main design philosophy in the Human-Computer interaction (HCI) field, making the need for culturally sensitive and responsive interfaces a major and critical issue in interactive design.

There is no doubt that in the context of globalization, culture and cultural identity are always considered important issues in all areas of life, including design activities. United Nations Educational, Scientific, and Cultural Organization (UNESCO) confirmed that designers often research and understand cultural perspectives to apply to their designs to create a connection between users and products, while enhancing the cultural identity of users [1]. A deep understanding of users' cultural identity is crucial in influencing design choices, ensuring that they are not only user-friendly but also culturally meaningful and emotionally appealing. In addition, Marcus and Gould [2] argued that culture plays an important role in shaping users' perceptions and interactions with digital products. Designs always aim to express the cultural nature of users. The concrete goal of achieving aesthetics, usefulness, and user experience always conceals the abstract goal [2].

Cultural identity is a complex set of values, beliefs, traditions, languages, and social practices that shape an individual or group's sense of belonging. In UI design, recognizing and integrating these cultural elements can improve the user experience (UX) by creating a deeper connection between the user and the digital product. Cultural identity with various elements such as values, beliefs, traditions, languages, and social customs... forms a sense of belonging for an individual or a group of people [1]. Applying this concept creatively in the field of UI/UX design, designers always try to embed these cultural elements (cultural identity) into their design products to form a deep and strong connection between users and digital products. Aesthetic design, functional design, and cultural communication design help users perceive, understand, and interact well with digital interfaces.

Interfaces must not only reflect technology but also be consistent with the cultural values, beliefs, and traditions of users. Therefore, studying and integrating cultural identity into UI design is necessary to create quality and effective user experiences. Exploring cultural identity in UI design involves considering factors such as language, religion, customs, and social practices. Cultural differences can greatly influence how users approach and use technology. This chapter explores the complex relationship between users' cultural identities and the reflective design styles used in creating interactive interfaces. In doing so, it demonstrates the need for culturally informed design practices.

1.2 Problem statement

In the context of the current industrial revolution 4.0 and globalization, UNESCO has repeatedly emphasized the importance of preserving and promoting cultural identity, affirming that globalization brings many opportunities but also poses great challenges to cultures around the world. To ensure increasing cultural diversity, the design of interactive user interfaces must not only meet users' needs in terms of functionality but also reflect the cultural identity of users. Therefore, it can be seen that cultural identity can affect the way users interact with the system. However, many designers and researchers still do not clearly understand the relationship between cultural identity and the design style reflected in interactive interfaces. As a result, interactive products have been created that do not meet users' needs, expectations, and experiences. Nowadays, understanding the cultural identity of users and applying them to the UI design process will be a key factor in shaping a reflective design style to create good digital experiences for users.

1.3 Research questions

- RQ1. What are the elements of user culture identity in UI design?
- RQ2. What factors of user culture identity affect Reflective Design Style?
- RQ3. How do reflective design methods based on user cultural identity?

This chapter aims to analyze and clarify the role of culture in general and user cultural identity in particular in reflective design style, with a special focus on UI design. By using an interdisciplinary approach and chapter structure, readers will have a better understanding of the relationship between culture and UI design style. Through qualitative research, the chapter will focus on analyzing concepts related to cultural identity and reflective design to better understand the relationship between them. Thereby, the chapter proposes a model for integrating user cultural identity into the UI design process. In addition, the chapter also proposes a method for shaping a more accessible and usable product design style, enhancing the user experience.

2. Literature review

In recent years, the study of the influence of cultural identity on the design style reflected in interactive user interfaces has attracted considerable attention from the academic and practical communities. This chapter's key concepts will offer a thorough understanding of culture, cultural identity, design style... An overview of the representative research works related to this topic will provide a comprehensive and in-depth view of this growing research area. The chapter contents select the literature review according to the following criteria:

Keywords and Search Phrases: Keywords can be a combination of terms and phrases that are directly related to the article's main concepts. Consider the terms "cultural identity," "design style," and "interactive user interface."

The chapter's contents search reliable databases for literature on design cultural studies and interactive design. The search is conducted using popular and reliable databases such as Google Scholar ACM Digital Library IEEE Xplore ScienceDirect SAGE Journals...

Articles that specifically mention cultural identity in the design context are examples of appropriate literature selection methods. Studies discussing reflective design or adaptive user interfaces; Studies published in peer-reviewed scientific journals or conferences, unless the older researches are fundamental, focus on recent publications. Articles provide empirical studies or theoretical frameworks on user-centered design, interaction design, and cultural diversity.

2.1 Culture and cultural identity in interface design

There are many definitions of culture in the social sciences. But the most standard and conventional reference that most cultural researchers in the world agree on is the definition of culture by the United Nations Educational, Scientific, and Cultural Organization (UNESCO). Culture is defined as "the set of distinctive spiritual, material, intellectual, and emotional features of society or a social group that encompasses, in addition to art and literature, lifestyles, ways of living together, value systems, traditions, and beliefs" [1]. This definition emphasizes the diversity and complexity of culture, including both tangible and intangible elements of social life, as well as the idea that culture is dynamic and constantly evolving. Culture includes the patterns, explicit and implicit, of and for behavior acquired and transmitted by symbols, which make up the distinctive achievements of human groups, including their embodiment in artifacts.

UNESCO's concept of culture serves as a basis for defining cultural identity and personal cultural identity. They also encompass the basic elements of culture. Gelfand et al. argues that in collectivist cultures, behavior is often driven by the need for harmony and social cohesion, while individualistic cultures encourage autonomy and creativity [3]. Wang et al. further investigate the differences in user expectations of interfaces, depending on their culture [4]. Nisbett and Masuda explore that differences in thinking between Eastern and Western cultures influence how technology is approached and used [5].

Personal cultural identity is a set of values, beliefs, and practices that characterize the culture to which an individual belongs, which has a profound influence on the way they interact with technology. Cultural factors such as users' values, beliefs, and technology usage habits can influence how users understand and interact with interfaces [2]. From the diverse definitions of culture and cultural identity, it can be determined that personal cultural identity is shaped by many different factors, from living environment to personal experiences and emotions as well as reflections of interactive activities in life. Tractinsky pointed out that the perception of interface aesthetics also differs across cultures [6]. The author of the study emphasized the importance of cultural identity in interface design. Cyr et al. also argued that cultural factors influence the reliability and aesthetics of interfaces [7]. Hofstede identified that individuality is an important component of cultural identity and it influences user behavior on digital interfaces [8]. Marcus and Gould in their study also emphasized the importance of customizing interfaces to match users' cultural norms and they also asserted that cultural language and symbols play an important role in how users perceive and interact with digital interfaces [2]. Reinecke and Bernstein also asserted that personalizing interfaces based on cultural characteristics can enhance user experience [9]. Choi et al. emphasized the role of education and access to technology in shaping user behavior [10]. Shen et al. emphasized that a deep understanding of individual cultural identity is an important factor in creating effective and accessible interactive user interfaces [11]. They argue that linguistic factors can influence the accessibility of interfaces to users from different cultures. In interface design, it is increasingly important to represent these cultural characteristics through visual media. UI design is also a way to reflect and highlight unique personal cultural values, providing a good user experience based on their personal identity.

2.2 Reflective design

The research direction of interaction design and reflective design was proposed from the research of Don Norman. He analyzed the design process to focus on meeting the needs and desires of users through comprehensive research about them. Then users become aware of their emotions or assumptions during the interaction with the product (1988). In the book "Emotional Design: Why We Love (or Hate) Everyday Things" [12], he once again affirmed the role of UI/UX design in shaping users' emotions and attitudes toward the product when interacting. He divided the design into three levels: (1) visceral level, (2) behavioral level, and (3) reflective level (**Figure 1**). He affirmed that design at the "reflective level" focuses on the meaning and value of the product to the individual user. Reflective design focuses on changing the way users think and feel, not only providing them with useful tools but also encouraging them to reflect on how they interact with the world around them, which is often overlooked by other design approaches such as User-Centered Design (UCD) or experience-based design.

In this direction, Sengers et al.'s study found that reflective design focuses on providing design considerations, encouraging users to think more deeply about their

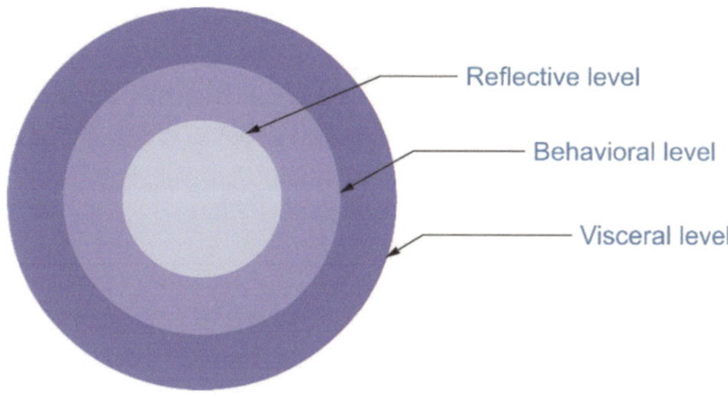

Figure 1.
Norman's three level of design.

experiences and to become more aware of the problems they face in their socio-cultural context [13]. This is different from the traditional design approach of simply meeting the functional needs of a product. Design is not simply about creating easy-to-use, beautiful interfaces but also focuses on enhancing the user's experience and expanding their awareness based on the user's cultural identity and cultural factors. In another study, Bardzell and Bardzell also pointed out that reflective design often encourages self-reflective and self-questioning interactions, as opposed to simply helping users to manipulate or providing solutions to problems they are facing [14].

In addition, Gaver et al. emphasized that reflective design does not necessarily adhere to strict usability principles but can intentionally create discomfort or conflict to promote reflection [15]. Whereas experience design focuses on creating rich and emotional experiences [16], reflective design focuses on provoking awareness of social and personal issues. Dourish also researched in art projects and cultural studies [17]. He asserts that the goal of a reflectively designed product is not to optimize performance but to promote reflection and change perception. This design often incorporates symbolic and expressive elements to convey a profound message [13]. Ford and Kotzé. studied the integration of cultural identity into user interface design through user research [18]. The study recommends user involvement in the design process to ensure that cultural elements are accurately reflected in the interface.

Some other studies suggest that interfaces at the reflective level should be able to be customized according to the user's culture. Therefore, they can improve product satisfaction and performance. Reinecke and Bernstein explore the ways in which cultural elements are expressed and their influence on user adaptation to adaptive user interfaces [9].

These studies have contributed to the formation and development of the concept of "Reflective Design Style," making it an important part of modern design theory. While design reflects cultural and personal nuances, an inseparable aspect of modern design is the user interface (UI). It can be generalized that Reflective Design is considered a user interface design method that reflects their inner selves and emotions or promotes their awareness/perception of their behaviors, values, and assumptions in the process of interacting with the product. Due to the comprehensiveness and effectiveness of "Reflective Design" in the fields of UI design, technology, and user experience, it has gradually become a popular research direction. When compared to User-Centered Design (UCD) methods, reflective design differs in that the design product does not necessarily optimize the user experience as in the traditional UCD design philosophy. Today's interactive interfaces play an important role in the digital experience process. Moreover, cultural values and messages are conveyed most directly on the interface. In addition to the aesthetics of interactive interface design (to make it beautiful), designers also aim to enhance the user experience, ensuring that messages and personal identity are reflected most effectively in each interactive product.

2.3 Interactive user interfaces

Interactive User Interface is a fundamental concept in software design and interactive technology. It acts as an intermediary between the user and the system, allowing the user to perform actions and receive feedback from the system in real time. Interactive user interfaces include elements such as images, sounds, and motions to create a smooth and engaging user experience [19]. The interface consists of many aspects. It is not only aesthetically pleasing, harmonious, and eye-catching, but it also has to be easy to use and friendly, meeting the user's tasks. Therefore, a good interactive interface will maximize communication efficiency. Shneiderman et al. asserted that usability and accessibility are two core factors in designing interactive user interfaces [20]. Lazar et al. emphasize that interactive user interface design is an iterative process that requires continuous evaluation and improvement based on user feedback [21]. Through interaction, users can perceive their comfort and experience. In the process of designing interactive interfaces, designers always need to rely on research on user behavior, expectations, goals, and needs to create natural and effective interactions [22].

In UI design, reflective design incorporates elements that adapt to user behavior and preferences. It encompasses a range of activities. Among them, building systems that can learn from user interactions and adapt to their needs over time. A design may adjust its layout based on user interaction patterns or suggest customization options based on user preferences and cultural identities. In the context of UI design, cultural identities play an important role in shaping our perceptions and interactions with the systems being designed. Reflective design can accommodate diverse cultural backgrounds by adapting to individual preferences and values. This may include incorporating language, visuals, or contextual interfaces that cater to specific cultural norms. The intersection of culture and UI design is not just a reflection but an interactive process where each element influences the other.

2.4 The influence of culture and user cultural identity on user interface design

The factors in interface design, such as the multicultural environment, the interplay between technology and culture, and the art of design, influence each other, promoting the formation of interface design styles. When studying their relationship and mutual influence, I will suggest designers create interfaces that reflect the cultural identity of the target users. Cultural identity is closely related to experience. Reinecke and Gajos demonstrate that not paying attention to cultural identity in design can lead to uncomfortable and difficult-to-use experiences [23]. Because different interface styles are understood and perceived in different cultures and therefore do not match the user's interaction perception, Callahan asserts that colors, icons, and layouts in interfaces need to be adjusted according to cultural standards to enhance user interaction and acceptance [24]. Smith et al. conducted a study that showed that cultural differences can influence design elements such as complexity, intuitiveness, and how information is presented [25]. Ford and Kotzé recommended that designers conduct culture-specific user studies to ensure that the interface is not only usable but also familiar and comfortable for users [26]. Differences in language and communication styles across cultures and how they influence interface design. Marcus and Gould [2] discussed the principles of cross-cultural user interface design, emphasizing the need to adapt designs to the cultural values and habits of users. Layout and interaction choices should be based on user research [27]. Nisbett and Masuda suggested that designers should also pay attention to the visual information processing factor of users [5]. Research confirms that culture affects users' perceptions and thinking, especially the difference between Eastern and Western cultures. The results show that users in different cultures will have different approaches and experiences when interacting with user interface systems. Therefore, affirming that personal cultural identity plays an important role in interactive user interface design, affecting the way users interact and experience digital systems. Once designers are aware that culture has a significant impact on the way users design user interfaces, the factors that cannot be ignored are usability and user experience (UX). In design, reflecting the culture and values of users well will make the interface easier to use and provide a smoother experience.

2.5 Usability and user experience

In the field of UI/UX design, studies have shown that users' cultural identity plays an important role in shaping the design styles reflected on interactive user interfaces. In the design process, in-depth research on cultural factors helps designers understand users better, and users' cultural identity is also highlighted, making a difference in design style choices. Furthermore, designers who integrate cultural factors into the design process will also help improve usability, creating a stronger emotional connection between users and digital products.

The research project of George et al. reaffirms that cultural aspects of Hofstede's cultural model affect human-computer interaction performance [28]. The study identified the test subjects and test interfaces based on cultural aspects, then analyzed and evaluated the impact of cultural factors on the interaction performance and task performance of users. The results of the study showed that usability varies across different cultural groups. The author asserted that to achieve this goal, it is necessary to (1) identify the characteristics of cultural aspects, (2) identify the test subjects and test interfaces that display appropriate cultural aspects, and (3) evaluate the impact of these cultural aspects on the speed, accuracy, and satisfaction that test subjects achieve when using the test interface to perform data collection tasks.

Also, with the idea of testing and evaluating how culture affects the user experience. Honold's study focused on examining how cultural factors influence the understanding and use of technological products [29]. The results showed that cultural awareness can significantly improve the usability and user satisfaction of digital interfaces. Hertzum synthesized and compared a number of interaction methods in different cultures to see the relationship between user cultural identity and interaction [30]. The research results are suggestions for design solutions suitable for each specific cultural context. The study shows the role and importance of cultural identity as well as the meaning of understanding users. Designers can apply cultural factors to create effective interactive interfaces. Aykin also collected studies and practical cases on multicultural user interface design in the context of globalization [31]. The author proposed some approaches to interaction design that take the user as the center and integrate cultural factors, user cultural identity into electronic interface design to bring users deep experiences.

When designing UI/UX, usability and user experience are two important basic elements that make up the success of interactive products. In addition, to deepen the interactive experience, designers also need to take into account other factors, such as the culture and cultural identity of users. Therefore, a design model that helps to approach users comprehensively is needed. This will help designers determine the design style more easily and make interface design more convenient and effective.

3. Reflective design based on user's cultural identity

3.1 Reflective design in user interface design

In the field of interaction design and user experience, Don Norman introduced the concept of "reflective design" and developed the reflective design theory [32]. In it, he emphasized the excellent experience that the product brings when designing interactive products. According to him, good design is not simply focusing on solutions to solve problems of function (usability) and aesthetics. Based on the philosophy of user-centered design, Norman's reflective design theoretical model divides design into three main levels: (1) Visceral level: the lowest and most common level of intuitive perception; (2) Behavioral level: the behavioral level often seen in interaction design, where products focus on usability and designers focus on solving the functional problem of the product; (3) Reflective level: the highest and deepest level of design. This is the level of reflection based on user experience.

In **Figure 1**, the reflective level refers to the personal feelings, thoughts, and meanings that users attach to a product. This means that the design must not only meet basic usage needs but also create deep connections, expressing value and meaning in the user's life. According to Norman, successful product design must not only create satisfaction during use but also leave a lasting impression, encouraging users to think about the product in a positive and meaningful way. From this perspective, design is not only an art but also a way to communicate and connect with users on a more subtle level. Designers need to do research to deeply understand users based on their needs and expectations. The message conveyed by the product also needs to evoke positive emotions. Most importantly, the reflections on the interactive product before, during, and after use. To do so, designers must conduct in-depth research on the culture and cultural identity of users to apply this to the design process.

3.2 Hofstede's Onion Model of Culture

In the field of cultural studies, Hofstede's Onion Model of Culture is a cultural analysis tool developed by Geert Hofstede. Hofstede's Onion Model of Culture can be understood as a hierarchical model, describing culture as an "onion" with many layers, from the external manifestations to the core values inside. This cultural model includes four main layers, corresponding to the four core elements that form culture. These are the outermost symbol layer, followed by the heroes layer, then the rituals layer, and the innermost, central layer, which is the values layer. These layers of elements are connected and expressed through human practical activities in the processes of labor, production, living activities, etc. According to this explanation, the user's personal cultural identity is also modeled in a similar way when superficial cultural elements (symbols, rituals) reflect the deep and core values that they have absorbed from the surrounding cultural environment. This personal cultural identity is reflected through the process of interacting with products and systems.

As mentioned above, the model describes culture as a multi-layered structure, like the layers of an onion. In the context of UI/UX design research, these layers specifically include:

1. *Symbols*: This is the outermost and most easily changed layer. Symbols include words, gestures, images, or objects that have specific meanings in a culture. Examples: national flags, traditional costumes, languages, etc.

2. *Heroes*: These are people, living or dead, who have noble qualities and are considered role models in the culture. Examples: leaders, historical figures, and entertainment stars.

3. *Rituals*: These are collective activities that are considered essential in a culture, although they may not have direct practical value; for example, festivals, religious ceremonies, and social customs.

4. *Values*: This is the deepest layer and the most difficult to change. Values are shared ideas about what is good, what is bad, what is right, and what is wrong in a society. They shape people's beliefs and attitudes.

Each layer of this model influences the other and helps explain how culture forms and changes. Hofstede's Onion Model helps us better understand the complexity and diversity of culture, as well as how cultural elements interact with each other in the product development process.

Based on the overall structure of culture (**Figure 2**), the cultural identity of an individual user (User Cultural Identity Model) can be deciphered using Hofstede's Onion Model of Culture (**Figure 3**). The layers of culture that a person interacts with and experiences can be analyzed by mapping the main elements of the cultural model

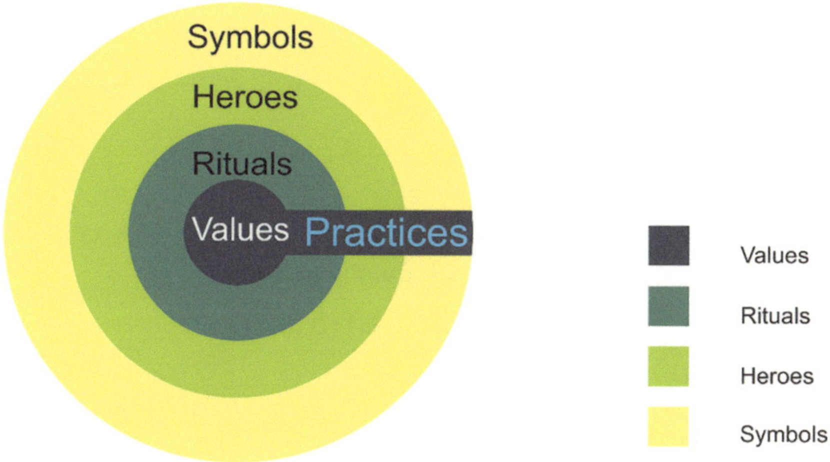

Figure 2.
Hofstede's Onion Model of Culture.

and a person's cultural identity. Here is how to apply this model to find out a person's cultural identity:

1. The Symbols layer is at the outermost of the interface. This is a cultural element. Therefore, users can recognize it. Designers can design based on the visceral design level. It includes visual elements (visually displayed on the interface); language (mother tongue and other languages that the person uses); clothing (how they dress every day and on special occasions); personal objects (objects or images with special meaning, such as national flags or cultural symbols).

2. The Heroes layer is the second that is hidden behind the icon (it is a synthesis of basic visual elements like in the Symbol layer) and helps create an additional layer of meaning for the interface, including historical figures (historical figures that the person admires or learns from); celebrities (entertainment stars, athletes, or influential people that they consider role models); family and friends (relatives, friends, or mentors who have a great impact on their lives and values).

3. The rituals layer is the third one. It is closely related to specific interaction methods (tasks) or non-verbal communication (gestures, eye contact, and other forms of non-verbal communication); festivals and holidays (cultural, religious, and national events that they participate in and celebrate); family rituals (family habits and traditions such as shared meals, weddings, and funerals); and daily routines (regular activities such as greetings, eating habits, and work habits).

4. The values layer is the central part of personal cultural identity and contains the good and characteristic values of a person. It includes: concepts of good and bad (things considered moral and immoral); personal values (honesty, fairness, respect for others); views on life (beliefs about the meaning of life, happiness, and success).

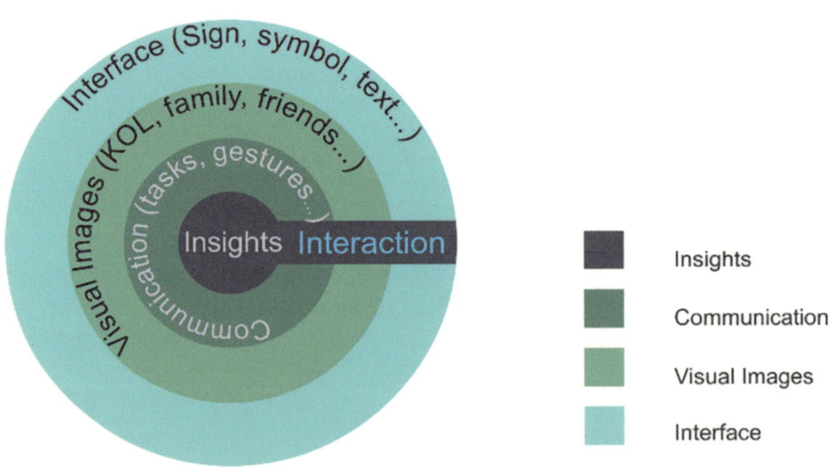

Figure 3.
The user cultural identity model based on Hofstede's Onion Model of Culture (Copyright by the author of the research).

Through the analysis of Hofstede's Onion Model of Culture, it is easy to see that designers need to rely on the connection between Norman's Three Level of Design (**Figure 1**) and User Cultural Identity Model (**Figure 3**) in the UI/UX design process. The symbols and images in the visual layer of the interface, along with the "rituals" (methods of operation), directly affect the way users perceive and interact with the interface. Designers simply need to design the visual at the visceral design level. For example, colors or icons in the interface can have different meanings in different cultures. Core values, located at the innermost (central) layer of the model, have the effect of shaping priorities and how users perceive, evaluate, and make decisions when using the interface at what level. Designers need to pay more attention to the highly abstract values expressed in the design at the reflective design level. Understanding this correlation helps designers create culturally appropriate products, enhance the user experience, and increase personalization in design [33].

The reflective design model is proposed based on User Cultural Identity (on the basis of a user-centered design philosophy) (**Figure 4**).

The bottom xOz is Hofstede's Onion Model of Culture (User Cultural Identity Model, expressing the idea that culture is the foundation, the root for developing all issues in UI/UX design).

The core part (O) is cultural values (highly abstract) that express the cultural identity of the user and have a highly reflective nature.

The further out in the x, y, or z direction toward the outermost layer, the more specific the image is (visually expressed on the UI interface).

The further up, the more abstract the design is and the more it expresses the user's personal cultural identity as well as its high reflection.

Table 1 shows the relationship between the user's cultural identity elements as well as how and how strongly they influence the design level.

Table 1 will help designers choose how to express a reflective design style quickly and effectively. All design elements (including user culture and cultural identity) need to be identified by listing them through a brainstorming session, and then the designer proceeds to categorize them into the corresponding cells of **Table 1**. Each cell is mapped to a specific column and row containing information about the design level

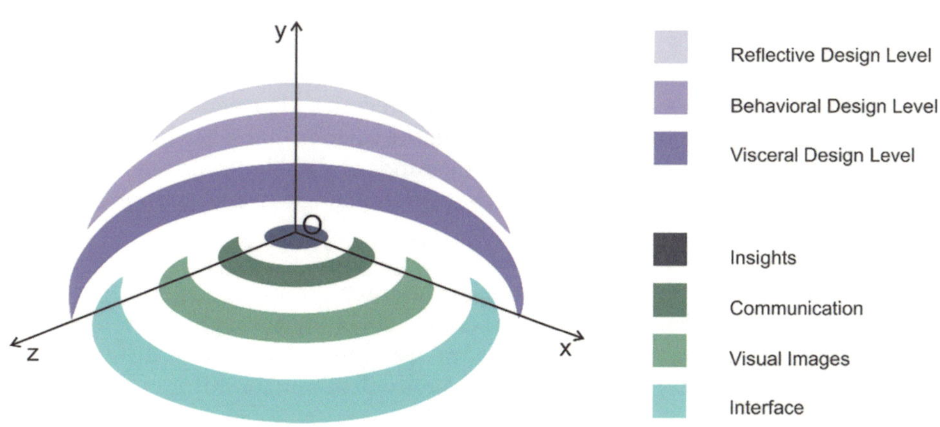

Figure 4.
The relationship between Norman's three level of design and user cultural identity based on Hofstede's Onion Model of Culture (Copyright by the author of the research).

	Values	Rituals	Heroes	Symbols
Reflective design	V-Rd	R-Rd	H-Rd	S-Rd
Behavioral design	V-Bd	R-Bd	H-Bd	S-Bd
Visceral design	V-Vd	R-Vd	H-Vd	S-Vd

Rd: Reflective design; V: Values; Bd: Behavioral design; R: Rituals; Vd: Visceral Design; H: Heroes; S: Symbols.

Table 1.
Relationship between elements of culture and design level. This comes up with table (4 columns x 3 rows) as 12 combinations.

(from visceral to reflection) and cultural layer (from symbol to value). In addition, it is important to note that the cultural diversity of users will also deeply and widely affect the process of designing a multicultural user interface. There are many different factors, such as visual elements (concrete, intuitive) or interaction methods and user experiences (abstract and highly reflective).

3.3 Case study exploring user cultural identity in shaping reflective design style on interactive user interfaces

The specific case analysis is a user interface of an interactive book product (Enabling the disabled children to learn Maths – **Figure 5**). By analyzing the relationship between design levels and elements of user cultural identity, we can see the level of combination and the level of influence of User cultural identity in shaping the graphic style of interface design.

To initiate the exploration of User Cultural Identity in the user interface, it is necessary to analyze the "Learning Central" interface using the dimensions of the User Cultural Identity Model, which is based on Hofstede's Onion Model of Culture.

- *Symbol layer (S)*: This is the outer layer of the interface. It includes visual elements such as spacecraft (classroom symbol), cartoon character (teacher symbol), icons, colors, and fonts. The interface features a cartoon-style teacher dressed in "modern superhero" costume, icons symbolizing various functions or subjects, and engaging fonts. The entire interface consistently employs a style suitable for children.

- *Heroes layer (H)*: This layer represents characters that represent the values of the system. Within the limits of this interface, the cartoon character in a superhero costume can be considered a hero (in the minds of disabled children, the teacher character is like flying in space to teach), symbolizing fun and excitement in learning.

- *Rituals layer (R)*: These are the activities and interactions that users engage in. For "Learning Central," rituals may include navigating through different functions/subjects, interacting with icons, and using buttons to access different educational content. The interaction process will stimulate children's interest in learning.

- *Values layer (V)*: The core layer, representing the principles and beliefs about learning experienced in the "Learning Central" environment. These values may

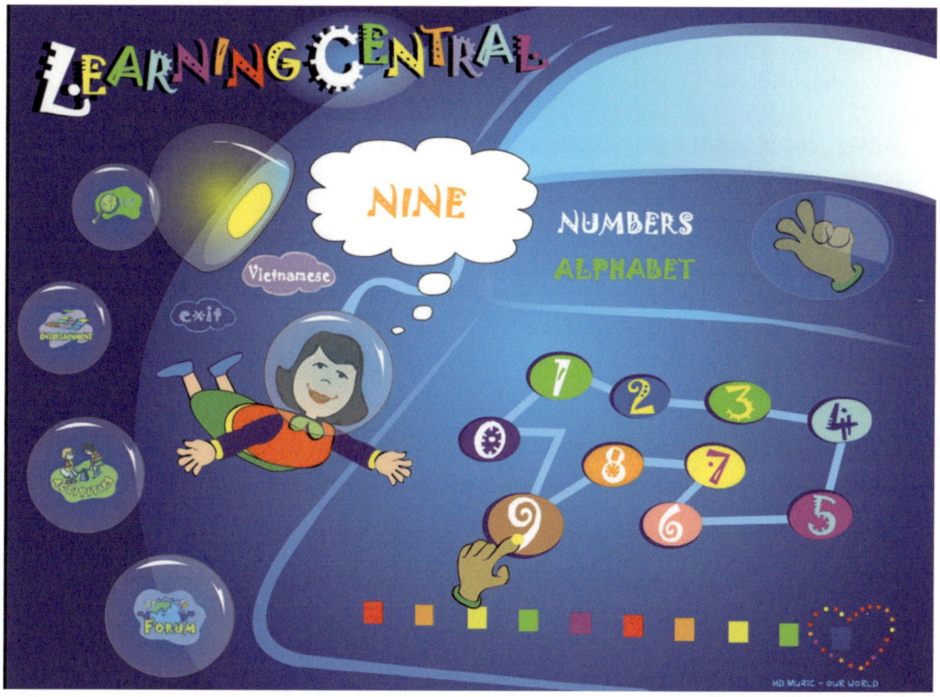

Figure 5.
Graphic User Interface – Enabling the disabled children Interactive book (Copyright by the author of the research).

focus on making learning fun and accessible for children, emphasizing interaction, participation, and a playful approach to learning.

Through analyzing these layers, we can understand how the "Learning Central" interface is designed to create an engaging and effective learning environment for children (considered in the User cultural identity layers).

The next step is to combine Norman's Three Levels of Design model with the User Cultural Identity model (based on Hofstede's Onion Model of Culture) to analyze the "Learning Central" user interface:

Visceral Design Level (Vd – specific design level, users can perceive visually):

- *Symbols (Vd-S)*: Visual elements such as cartoon characters (teachers), symbols, icons, colors, and fun fonts create a strong and attractive first impression for children.

- *Heroes (Vd-H)*: Hero character (flying teacher in the spaceship classroom) in brightly colored costumes creates a sense of fun and stimulates the curiosity of disabled children. All the time, they wish to fly like the hero-teacher.

Behavioral Design Level (Bd – Designing behavior through the interaction and navigation process of children as they experience learning):

- *Rituals (Bd-R)*: An easy-to-use interface with clear navigation buttons and recognizable icons makes it easy for children to interact and learn. Activities such as selecting functions or subjects and using buttons to access educational content pose a big problem for designers when they want to meet the needs of children with disabilities.

- *Values (Bd-V)*: Focus on making learning fun and accessible, helping children feel comfortable and confident when using the interface.

Reflective Design Level (Rd – Reflective design is difficult to perceive visually. It is abstract to be able to design. Children can only feel it through their attachment to the experience and lessons from the interactive product):

- *Values (Rd-V)*: The interface helps children learn Maths and creates lasting memories and impressions of learning.

- *Heroes (Rd-H)*: Superhero – flying teachers can be symbol of success and joy in learning, creating an emotional connection with children.

It is possible to better understand how to design the "Learning Central" interface to create a comprehensive and engaging learning experience for children with disabilities based on their identity by combining both models with the combinations (**Table 1**). In other words, the analysis allows us to see how the user's identity has influenced the design of the interactive interface.

4. Conclusion

In the context of globalization and the continuous development of technology, integrating the cultural identity of users into the design style reflected on interactive user interfaces has become an important factor. If this can be done in the process of designing interactive products, we can ensure the usability and emotional engagement of users in the process of interacting with computers. In-depth research on cultural factors in general and the cultural identity of users in particular not only helps create friendly user interfaces but also brings rich and diverse user experiences. Thereby contributing to the creation of digital products that both achieve aesthetics and ensure usability as well as a good experience. Interfaces will truly reflect the diversity and richness of cultures around the world.

Culture in general and the cultural identity of users in particular are discussed and analyzed in depth in the book chapter, clarifying the relationship between the cultural identity of users and design style, as well as their strong influence on reflective design elements. The arrangement of visual elements in interfaces is done in a manner that is both aesthetically pleasing and functional, while also incorporating profound cultural symbolism. Through the implementation of reflective design, they have the ability to establish culturally significant connections with users and elicit various emotional reactions from them.

During the early stages of interface development, designers need to prioritize user research to inform decisions about graphic style to be used. The layout of visual cues, from generic images and icons to specific elements like color and shape, reflects the users' cultural identity. They need to ensure that cultural factors are important when creating interactions and user experiences for individuals from diverse global backgrounds. Therefore, misaligning design decisions with users' cultural identities can result in misunderstandings or even negative reactions during system interactions. In fact, designers can create many beautiful and attractive interfaces. However, not all designers are successful in designing interfaces that are suitable for multicultural user contexts. A skillful combination of design levels (from visceral design to inflective design) will make the interface more professional and profound.

Research on cultural identity and reflective design style promises to make important contributions to creating personalized designs and enhancing emotional connections with users in HCI. The book chapter raises expectations: a deeper understanding of cultural identity and its influence on design creativity, creating personalized reflective designs, and designing UIs that are global but still retain the characteristics and quintessence of each culture. In addition, the book chapter also opens up future directions: developing and expanding existing theories on cultural identity and reflective design, creating new theoretical frameworks in graphic design, etc., making important contributions to the development of sustainable design philosophy, understanding and respecting cultural diversity in today's world, as well as forming effective interaction design guidelines.

Author details

Nguyen Duc Son[1,2]

1 FPT – Greenwich Vietnam University, Ho Chi Minh City, Vietnam

2 Graphic Design Department, Greenwich, Vietnam

*Address all correspondence to: sonnd24@fe.edu.vn

References

[1] UNESCO Framework for Culture Statistics [Internet]. Available from: https://uis.unesco.org/sites/default/files/documents/unesco-framework-for-cultural-statistics-2009-en_0.pdf [Accessed: 10 August 2024]

[2] Marcus A, Gould E. Crosscurrents: cultural dimensions and global Web user-interface design. Interactions. 2000;7:32-46

[3] Gelfand M, Bhawuk D, Nishii L, Bechtold D. Individualism and collectivism. In: The International Encyclopedia of Intercultural Communication. Sage Publications, Inc.; 2004. pp. 437-512

[4] Wang FP, Gale JFW. Screening criteria for shale-gas systems. Gulf Coast Association of Geological Societies Transaction. 2009;**59**:779-793

[5] Nisbett R, Masuda T. Culture and point of view. Proceedings of the National Academy of Sciences of the United States of America. 2003;**100**:11163-11170

[6] Tractinsky N. Aesthetics and apparent usability: empirically assessing cultural and methodological issues. In: Proceedings of the ACM SIGCHI Conference on Human factors in computing systems [Internet]. New York, NY, USA: Association for Computing Machinery; 1997. pp. 115-122. DOI: 10.1145/258549.258626

[7] Cyr D, Head M, Larios H. Colour appeal in website design within and across cultures: A multi-method evaluation. The International Journal of Human-Computer Studies. 1 Jan 2010;**68**(1):1-21

[8] Hofstede G. Culture's Consequences: Comparing Values, Behaviors, Institutions and Organizations Across Nations [Internet]. [cited 2024 Aug 20]. Available from: https://www.researchgate.net/publication/230557580_Culture's_Consequences_Comparing_Values_Behaviors_Institutions_and_Organizations_Across_Nations [Accessed: 20 August 2024]

[9] Reinecke K, Bernstein A. Knowing What a User Likes: A Design Science Approach to Interfaces that Automatically Adapt to Culture. MIS Quarterly. 2013;**37**(2):427-453

[10] Choi J, Lee HJ, Sajjad F, Lee H. The influence of national culture on the attitude towards mobile recommender systems. Technological Forecasting and Social Change. 2014;**86**:65-79

[11] Shen ST, Woolley M, Prior S. Towards culture-centred design. Interacting with Computers. 2006;**18**(4):820-852

[12] Norman DA. Emotional Design: Why We Love (or Hate) Everyday Things. New York: Basic Books; 2004. pp. 63-98

[13] Sengers P, Boehner K, David S, Kaye JJ. Reflective Design. Ithaca, NY, USA: Culturally Embedded Computing Group, Cornell Information Science; 2005. pp. 49-58. DOI: 10.1145/1094562.1094569

[14] Bardzell J, Bardzell S. Conclusion. In: Bardzell J, Bardzell S, editors. Humanistic HCI [Internet]. Cham: Springer International Publishing; 2015. pp. 143-146. DOI: 10.1007/978-3-031-02214-2_7

[15] Gaver WW, Boucher A, Pennington S, Walker B. Cultural probes and the value of uncertainty. Interactions. 2004;**11**(5):53-56

[16] Wright P, Wallace J, McCarthy J. Aesthetics and experience-centered design. ACM Transactions on Computer-Human Interaction. 2008;**15**(4):18:1-18:21

[17] Dourish P. Implications for design. In: Proceedings of the SIGCHI Conference on Human Factors in Computing Systems [Internet]. New York, NY, USA: Association for Computing Machinery; 2006. pp. 541-550. DOI: 10.1145/1124772.1124855

[18] Ford G, Kotzé P, Marcus A. Cultural dimensions: Who is stereotyping whom. In: Proc 11th Int Conf Hum-Comput Interact. 1 Jan 2005

[19] Benyon D. Designing Interactive Systems: A Comprehensive Guide to HCI, UX and Interaction Design. Pearson; 2013. p. 604

[20] Shneiderman B. Human-Centered Artificial Intelligence: Three Fresh Ideas. AIS Transactions on Human-Computer Interaction. 2020;**12**(3):109-124

[21] Lazar J, Feng JH, Hochheiser H. Research Methods in Human-Computer Interaction. US: Morgan Kaufmann of Elsevier; 28 Apr 2017. p. 562

[22] Norman K, Kirakowski J. The Wiley Handbook of Human Computer Interaction Set. Vol. 2. USA: John Wiley and Sons; 2017. p. 1043

[23] Reinecke K, Gajos KZ. Quantifying visual preferences around the world. In: Proceedings of the SIGCHI Conference on Human Factors in Computing Systems. [Internet]. 2014. DOI: 10.1145/2556288.2557052

[24] Callahan E. Cultural similarities and differences in the design of university web sites. Journal of Computer-Mediated Communication. Nov 2005;**11**(1):239-273

[25] Smith PB, Bond MH. Cultures and persons: Characterizing national and other types of cultural difference can also aid our understanding and prediction of individual variability. Frontiers in Psychology. 2019;**10**:2-7. Available from: https://www.frontiersin.org/journals/psychology/articles/10.3389/fpsyg.2019.02689/full [Accessed: 20 August 2024]

[26] Ford G, Kotzé P. Designing Usable Interfaces with Cultural Dimensions. In: Costabile MF, Paternò F, editors. Human-Computer Interaction-INTERACT 2005 [Internet]. Berlin, Heidelberg: Springer Berlin Heidelberg; 2005. pp. 713-726. (Lecture Notes in Computer Science; vol. 3585). Available from: http://link.springer.com/10.1007/11555261_57 [Accessed: 20 August 2024]

[27] Marcus A. Cultural Dimensions and Global Web User-Interface Design: What? So What? Now What?

[28] George K, Ave D, Africa S, Za A, Gelderblom H, et al. The effects of culture on performance achieved through the use of human computer interaction. In: SAICSIT '03: Proceedings of the 2003 Annual Research Conference of the South African Institute of Computer Scientists and Information Technologists on Enablement through Technology. 2003. pp. 218-230

[29] Honold P. Culture and Context: An Empirical Study for the Development of a Framework for the Elicitation of Cultural Influence in Product Usage. International Journal of Human Computer Interaction. 2000;**12**: 327-345

[30] Hertzum M, Hornbæk K, Shi Q, Yammiyavar P. Cultural cognition in usability evaluation. Interact Computers. 1 Jul 2009;**21**:212-220

[31] Aykin N. Usability and Internationalization of Information Technology. London: CRC Press, Laurence Erlbaum Associates; 2004. p. 393

[32] Norman D. The Design of Everyday Things

[33] Nguyen Duc Son. The Art of Interactive and User Interface Design. Vietnam: Fine Arts Publishing House; 2018

Chapter 4

Eye Physiology, Movement, and the Role of Eye Tracking in Instructional Design

Arwa Mashat

Abstract

Eye tracking has been used for several decades in various disciplines to measure eye movements, assess workload, gauge consumer preferences, and adapt systems for human interactions. It is used with increased frequency in instructional research to assess visual attention and interaction during learning while linking to other physiological, perception, and cognitive measures. This chapter comprehensively describes eye tracking for instructional research, design, and development. This chapter will present a historical overview of the development of eye tracking, as many of the early systems were focused on research and development. Still, over time, the equipment to measure eye movements has become more commonplace, more accurate, and less expensive, while the complex algorithms to measure eye movements have become more effective and efficient and leverage increases in computing power to provide real-time information. Today, eye tracking is possible through dedicated research-based eye-tracking systems, as well as *via* embedded technologies in a variety of consumer devices such as mobile phones, computer-based web cameras, and wearable technologies, including smart glasses, where the technology supports measuring eye movements, adapting interfaces, and augmenting reality to support training and enhance work performance. This makes eye tracking a viable and valuable tool for instructional research and as an embedded tool for instruction that already utilizes these systems.

Keywords: eye tracking, instructional design, visual attention, human interaction, measuring eye movements

1. Introduction

The human eye is a complex organ that plays a vital role in our ability to perceive the world around us. Knowledge of its physiological nature, movement, and the process of seeing itself will prove immensely helpful in how such elements relate to behavior and cognitive processing. This chapter overview shows the knowledge of eye physiology, the mechanism of eye movements, and how these processes are interrelated with visual attention and learning. This chapter summarizes the current applications of eye-tracking technology, emphasizing instruction and how it may be leveraged to improve education outcomes.

Eye tracking has been used for many years in different activities: psychology, medical studies, user experience design, and many others. The first eye tracker devices at the beginning of the twentieth century included contact lenses with attached pointers. Further on, light beams began to be used to track eye reflections on film; by the 1960s, this approach had been considerably improved by the development of modern eye-tracking methods [1].

The section covers the physiology of the eye, going into great detail about the anatomical structure: the cornea, pupil, lens, and retina. Each of them works in unison to constitute the vision of an organism. There are two main types of eye movements: fixations and minor stops, where the gaze is focused on one point saccade, which are jumps along different fixation points. The viewing process involves light entering the eye and being focused on the retina through the lens; photoreceptors change the light into neural signals, and the brain processes these [1].

1.1 Anatomy of the eye

The human eye comprises several essential structures that work together to make vision possible. The cornea and lens focus light onto the retina, where photoreceptor cells (rods and cones) convert the light to neural signals. The retina sends these signals to the brain through the optic nerve, which allows us to perceive visual information [2].

It will include the physiological details about the eye and cognitive processes that interpret visual stimuli. Visual attention is a mechanism that enables one to focus on specific aspects of one's surroundings while paying less attention to others. This selective attention relates to cognitive load, the mental effort to process information [3].

Eye physiology refers to the complex anatomy and physiology of the eyes, which are crucial for human vision.

The general anatomy of the eye (see **Figure 1**) includes the following:

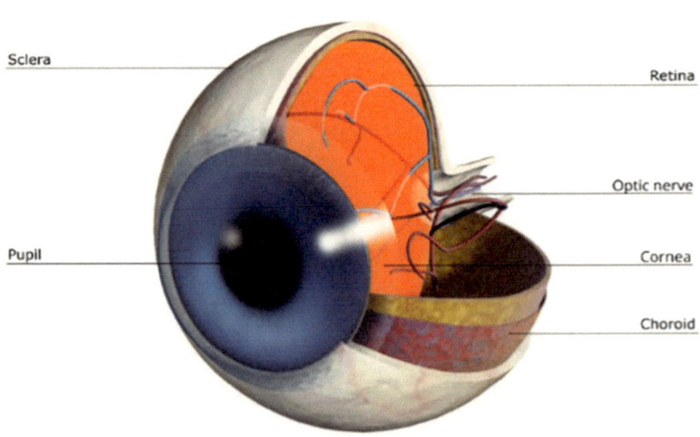

Figure 1.
Anatomy of the eye.

DOI: http://dx.doi.org/10.5772/intechopen.1008301

- The cornea is the transparent frontal layer through which light enters the eye, undergoing refraction.
- *Iris and pupil*: The iris controls the amount of light that enters through the regulation of pupil size. The pupil is the central opening of the iris.
- *Lens*: Behind the pupil, the lens focuses light on the retina with the help of changing shape; the process is called accommodation.
- *Retina*: This is the innermost layer with photoreceptors, which change light into electrical signals.
- *Optic nerve*: It transmits visual information from the retina to the brain.

Seeing starts with light entering the eye through the cornea, pupil, and lens, and focusing on the retina. Rods and cones detect light inside the retina and convert it into electrical impulses. *Via* the optic nerve, the impulses reach the visual cortex in the brain, where they are processed into images.

1.2 Measures in eye tracking

These movements form part of how we visually scan the environment and are crucial for understanding visual attention and cognitive processing. Eye movements can be differentiated into a few types of quantitative measures, such as the following:

- Saccades are fast eye movements that shift gaze from one fixation point to another. They help us scan the environment and gather information about it. Shorter saccades may indicate that the person is more thorough in his information examination, while longer ones may suggest the reverse of engagement.
- *Fixations*: Small stops of the eyes where visual information is elaborated. The duration and place of these fixations reflect visual attention. Cognitive processing is linked to a longer duration and is generally viewed as a more profound engagement with the material.
- *Pupillometry*: Pupil dilations may reflect cognitive load; for instance, larger pupils have more often than not been interpreted as indicative of increased mental effort [4].
- *Pursuit movements*: Smooth tracking movements that allow the eyes to follow moving objects.

These movements are crucial in guiding the attentional gaze and relate to cognition. An "eye-mind assumption" purports that eye movements reveal certain moments of cognitive processing; the eyes move to the information one is processing [5]. Eye movements can, therefore, be used to assess an individual's activity in processing information, decision-making, and interaction with the environment. These metrics allow instructors to tailor instructional content to meet learners' needs best and provide accessible and engaging content.

There is a meaningful relationship between eye movement and behavior regarding cognitive processing. For example, the duration of fixations when one reads is related to the difficulty of the material processed. Indeed, eye-tracking experiments show that more extended fixation typically indicates a more significant cognitive load and deeper engagement in the material covered.

The physiology of the eye underlines the mechanics of vision, and eye movements have been used as an index of cognitive processes that reflect an individual's attention and information processing. Researching these relations will benefit educational practices and the usability of user interfaces in technology [6, 7].

1.3 Eye-tracking hardware devices

The working principle of eye tracking has dramatically improved, with the variants in equipment that include:

- *Remote eye trackers* are fixed devices that may track eye movements from a distance. They are accurate but restrict head movement. They work while tracking the movements of the eyes without physical contact.

- *Mobile eye trackers* would enable the range of movement and allow naturalistic settings, but they can also be bulky and more expensive. These wearable devices can be worn over one's glass. They enable tracking in real-world environments, therefore offering ecological validity.

Mobile eye trackers include smart glasses that users can wear to track their eye movements in real-world settings. Smart glass is based on making a pair of wearable eyeglasses with embedded eye-tracking technology. Most models use video-based methods of acquiring eye movements and gaze direction; such methods allow a natural field of view for the user. The smart glasses contain web cameras to capture video from the user's eyes. These cameras are usually set to track both eyes, providing information about eye movements such as fixation and saccades. In addition, IR LEDs are generally deployed around the eyes to illuminate them and create reflections on the cornea. These reflections, together with the position of the pupil, are used in calculating gaze direction. The video data captured would be processed using algorithms that analyze the relationship between the position of the pupil and the corneal reflections. This is utilized to deduce the point of gaze relative to the environment or the displayed content, for example, on a screen. In general, a calibration process ensures the precision of how a user looks at known points on a display to collate the eye-tracking data with actual visual stimuli being looked at. Together, these features enable smart glasses to facilitate a panoramic view of where the wearer is looking in real time, which is applicable in many fields, including education, user experience research, medicine, and others.

- *Chin-up systems*: These systems stabilize the head; however, doing so may limit the natural movement of the eyes and hence affect the accuracy of data obtained in dynamic situations [1]. Measurements within eye tracking typically record the position and/or movement of the eyes for analyzing visual attention and cognitive processes.

1.4 Eye-tracking software and algorithms

It involves a set of algorithms for processing the raw data the hardware captures. Many algorithms will be applied to examine gaze patterns, fixation points, and saccade dynamics. Software applications are subject to significant variation in quality when it comes to data interpretation and analysis [1]. Eye-tracking algorithms can analyze these data for critical metrics, such as fixation points and saccades. Most software packages include analysis software that allows the researcher to visually depict the eye movement data through heat maps and gaze plots, facilitating much easier result interpretation [2].

Among the advantages of remote eye trackers are ease of use and installation, whereas their disadvantages lie in limited mobility. On the other hand, mobile eye trackers can provide flexibility and allow more natural viewing; they may involve higher costs and complexity in data processing. Software and algorithms also differ depending on the research needs. Some have been designed with high accuracy for clinical applications, while others focus on speed for real-time analysis in interactive environments [1].

1.5 Types of eye-tracking measurement techniques

The earlier eye trackers, such as those with analog video, relied on manual calibration, focusing, and positioning adjustments. By contrast, modern devices often employ auto-focusing cameras, self-calibration features, and digital communication protocols [2].

- *Accuracy and calibration*: Modern video-based eye trackers can achieve an accuracy of about 0.5 degrees and self-calibrate, making them user-friendly. In the past, systems required lengthy calibration and more cumbersome setups [2].

- *Portability vs. usability*: Head-mounted systems are wearable and offer mobility, especially in dynamic environments. In contrast, table-mounted systems generally are mounted on a table and provide higher accuracy within a controlled environment. One choice usually depends on what is being measured or required from an application [2].

- *Sampling rates*: These differ from sampling rates for other devices, which could still impart variations in data quality. Higher-level trackers may sample at 2000 Hz, while others sample as low as 50 Hz. Applications that require high temporal measurement precision prefer higher sampling rates [8].

- *Electro-oculography (EOG)*: This technique is based on the electric potential differences around the eye, measured by placing active electrodes around the eye area. It was one of the earliest methods, but it can only measure eye movements relative to head position, thus restricting its use for point-of-regard measurements only if combined with head tracking [2].

- *Scleral contact lens/search coil*: A contact lens with an embedded coil measures eye movement. Although the measurement is sensitive, it is invasive [2].

- *Photo-oculography (POG) and video-oculography (VOG)*: These techniques track visible features of the eye, such as the position of the pupil and limbus. They are usually noninvasive; however, they may require manual analysis of video recordings, which is cumbersome and prone to error [2].

- *Video-based combined pupil/corneal reflection*: This modern approach uses inexpensive cameras and image processing to obtain real-time eye position measurements. This latter technique has recently become popular for human-computer interaction studies as it is noninvasive and can function in real time [2].

2. Eye-tracking methodologies: Overview and applications

Eye-tracking technology has evolved dramatically and offers several methods to analyze visual attention, cognitive processes, and user interactions in education, psychology, human-computer interaction (HCI), and marketing. Some earlier works by Yarbus [9] demonstrated how task demands could influence eye movements, emphasizing visual attention for cognitive processing [2]. Integration of the cognitive load theory [3] explains a framework of how complexities of tasks influence cognitive load and, thus, eye movement behavior [2].

Advances in eye-tracking technology have led to the development of more accurate and user-friendly devices, thus making them more accessible for various applications. Such systems allow for video-based eye tracking, real-time gaze pattern analysis, and visual attention analysis [2].

The application of eye-tracking methodology in educational research makes a far-reaching contribution to our insight into the cognitive processes that appear during learning. Eye-tracking technology enables the investigation of how learners engage in educational material by recording eye movements that may indicate the distribution of attention and strategies of cognitive processing. For instance, in one of the studies on the efficiency of different computer-supported learning strategies, it was identified that graphic organizers facilitated the generative learning strategies by significantly increasing the up-down transitions between paragraphs of the text, as compared to full traditional reading of a text. This finding points to the importance of instructional strategies that actively engage students with the material, as documented by higher comprehension test scores for participants using graphic organizers or combined strategies such as highlighting and note-taking.

More to the point, no linear reading approaches typical in traditional methods of approaching the text, such as highlighting and note-taking, provide for deeper cognitive processing because eye movements and comprehension scores have been similar to those in the control group [10]. A combination of multiple learning strategies results in deeper cognitive engagement, that is, the finding through greater transitions in eye movements and superior retention on memory tests [2]. Therefore, eye tracking has become an essential tool in establishing the efficiency of educational intervention through the detailed patterns it shows in the way learners get engaged and comprehend the material, which again informs best practices in instructional design. These findings indicate that graphic organizers are more effective than other means of facilitating comprehension [2]. It has been used in HCI to evaluate the usability of interfaces, where researchers study user gaze to develop better interface designs. Advanced techniques, such as gaze-contingent displays, have been developed to provide users with an interactive environment that responds to user attention [2]. Different studies have indicated how gaze-based interaction can enrich users' experiences and effectiveness in digital environments [2, 11].

Eye-tracking marketing research is about understanding consumer behavior. It considers eye gaze in the analysis of advertisements. The resultant studies indicated a case of "banner blindness," in which users seem to miss the banner ads whether it is there or not [2]. The "F" pattern of visual attention in web searches shows how a user usually scans the content, guiding the strategy for placing ads [2]. Visualization is important when designing an advertisement or instructional material for learners. Users' attention can make a difference in the outcomes of learning or even marketing [12].

In summary, eye tracking can narrow the gap between cognitive psychology and educational methods. In other words, it will provide researchers with more insight into how various learning strategies influence cognitive processes when analyzing eye movement data; it will thus enhance educational practices to meet the diverse needs of learners best. With further development, this technology holds the potential for broader investigation within multiple educational contexts to extend insights into the complex interplay of cognition and learning.

3. Eye tracking in instructional design research and instructional systems

Many studies have been related to applying eye tracking in an instructional context. For instance, using a meta-analysis of research into eye movements and learning [7] identified a series of themes around eye movement, including information processing patterns and effects of instructional designs. These studies support how eye tracking can be used to enhance the designs of multimedia learning and instructional strategies in these areas [13].

Accordingly, eye-tracking technology has gained traction in educational research because it provides insight into how learners interact with instructional materials. Such a technology allows one to measure an individual's visual attention, cognitive load, and processing efficiency; hence, it offers exciting performance variables that may inform instructional design. Eye movements are linked with behavior and cognitive processes. Investigating eye movements can help designers determine the user's visual attention [12]. It has been demonstrated in studies that patterns of eye movements, such as fixation duration and frequency, may reveal information about mental load and decision-making processes, and even emotional states: Longer fixations could signal higher cognitive effort or interest [14]; rapid saccades might suggest distraction or search for information [1]. Eye tracking has been exceedingly helpful in researching cognition, which includes attention and memory. Eye movements indicate underlying cognitive strategies when problem solving [5, 15].

The integration of eye tracking into cognitive neuroscience has made it possible to understand how the brain processes visual information [16]. Using eye tracking makes it possible to objectively measure the process through which visual attention evolves with the fluctuation of cognitive load and expertise, and hence, it is a valuable tool with great potential for informing insights in learning processes [7].

Researchers should consider the reliability of their measures to ensure the validity of results in eye-tracking studies. One effective method is cross-validation, which involves incorporating eye-tracking data with other physiological measures. Additionally, conducting longitudinal studies that track eye movements can help identify patterns and trends related to learning processes, further enhancing the robustness of the findings.

Eye tracking has become one of the main instruments of instructional design research, allowing researchers to explore the cognitive processes beneath learning. Employing eye tracking, one can perceive how learners navigate educational materials and what they give priority to during navigation to appraise instructional strategies. For example, research has documented that eye-tracking measures, such as the length or number of fixations, may indicate learner engagement and comprehension levels. This would, in turn, allow for further insight into how the learners process information and enable the construction of more efficient instructional systems that address the needs of every individual. Furthermore, eye tracking can provide helpful input for developing adaptive learning environments that may change the contents dynamically depending on the learners' visual attention patterns. Such practice could eventually lead to an improvement in the whole learning process. Indeed, embedding eye-tracking technology into the instructional design would stimulate research into cognitive load and attention; it also allowed the structured development of personalized learning experiences congruent with the cognitive architecture of the students. In this regard, eye tracking in educational contexts may rise to the realization that it improves instructional design by bridging the gap between theoretical insights and practical applications using empirical data from visual attention and learning dynamics. This adaptability further enhances engagement and addresses the variance in cognitive load each student faces. As eye-tracking technology advances and becomes easier to use, its application within instructional design will continue to increase, encouraging creative teaching and learning methods for a wide range of educational areas. It is, therefore, a frontier in educational research, bridging the gaps between cognitive psychology and instructional design to improve educational practice.

4. Advantages and disadvantages of eye tracking

Eye-tracking technology has several advantages and disadvantages that researchers and practitioners should consider:

- Advantages:
  - *Objective measurement*: The eye-tracking technique provides objective and quantitative data on where and how long a person looks at given stimuli, allowing the researcher to conduct a practical analysis of visual attention and cognitive processes [8].
  - *Noninvasive-most of the state-of-the-art eye-tracking systems, particularly* video-based, operate non-contact with the participant. That is why they result in more comfort for the participant who wears these [2].
  - *High-temporal resolution*: Eye trackers can capture saccades and fixations while eye movements are rapid, offering insight into cognitive processes unfolding in real time [8].
  - *Wide-ranging applications*: Eye tracking finds its applications in a wide range of areas, starting with psychology, then marketing and usability testing, education, and medical research. It enhances our knowledge of visual processing and user interaction [8].
- Disadvantages:
  - *Calibration issues*: Most eye trackers require a calibration phase before being used, which may be time-consuming and only sometimes effective for all respondents because of some other shapes or conditions of the eye [6].

- *Precise calibration* is required to get valuable data; however, several factors, such as participant variability, can easily affect this.

- *Data quality variability*: Eye-tracking data may be affected due to the properties of ambient light in a setting, participant movement, or even by wearing glasses, thus showing variabilities in the data quality [8].

- *Midas touch problem*: The problem occurs when gaze input causes accidental actions; merely looking at an object may turn it on, which creates interface design problems [17].

- *Limited peripheral vision capture*: Most eye-tracking measures focal vision fovea, and peripheral visual attention needs to be captured more. This limits the understanding of holistic visual processing [6].

- *Cost and complexity*: Despite decreasing prices, high-end eye trackers will remain expensive shortly. Technical competence may be needed for installation and integration with the experimental designs [2].

- *Data interpretation*: The association between eye movements and underlying cognitive processes may sometimes be nontrivial and needs detailed analysis and specific contextual information.

In summary, while eye tracking offers significant advantages for understanding visual attention and cognitive processes, it also comes with challenges that must be managed to ensure accurate and meaningful data collection.

5. Future directions for eye tracking

While eye-tracking technology is still likely to develop further, so are its applications in educational contexts. In the future, for instance, this could be extended to adaptive learning systems. Eye tracking integrated into intelligent tutoring systems can yield personalized learning experiences that adapt dynamically to visual attention and cognitive load [18]. In addition to formal and informal learning settings, eye tracking can be utilized in traditional classrooms and extend to online learning platforms to extend our understanding of how learners engage with content.

The research is moving toward more robust and versatile eye-tracking systems capable of integrating into naturalistic settings, which permits investigating social interaction and learning processes in naturalistic situations [2].

Future research may consider how interdisciplinary collaborations can further apply eye tracking within various disciplines, including those in assistive technologies and virtual reality [2].

Eye tracking is an interdisciplinary research instrument that bridges the gap between various scientific disciplines. Due to continuous technology and methodological advancements, it has more significant potential for further insights into human cognition, user experience, and behavioral patterns.

6. Conclusion

Eye tracking provides a robust tool for capturing information relative to visual attention, cognitive processing, and learning in instructional situations. Educators will be informed about exactly how students engage with materials and will be able to refine instructional design based on this to optimize learning outcomes. In this respect, the potential of eye-tracking information on educational practices is expected to expand further as technology develops. This would lay concrete pathways toward more effective and personalized learning experiences.

This chapter concludes that eye-tracking technology plays a significant role in understanding cognitive processes, user experience, and user interactions in various domains. Ongoing improvements in eye-tracking systems, algorithms, and analytical tools ensure the further extension of their applications in education, medicine, and behavioral research.

The choice of an eye-tracking device will depend on the specific needs of the research or application to be served, including the required accuracy, environment, and whether the system needs to be portable or stationary. Each method and type of device presents trade-offs regarding invasiveness, accuracy, and user experience.

Author details

Arwa Mashat
Faculty of Computing and Information Technology, King Abdulaziz University, Rabigh, Saudi Arabia

*Address all correspondence to: aasmashat@kau.edu.sa

References

[1] Mikhailenko M, Maksimenko N, Kurushkin M. Eye-tracking in immersive virtual reality for education: A review of the current progress and applications. In: Frontiers in Education. Vol. 7. Switzerland: Frontiers Media SA; 2022. p. 697032

[2] Duchowski AT. Eye Tracking Methodology: Theory and Practice. Switzerland: Springer International Publishing; 2017

[3] Sweller J. Cognitive load during problem solving: Effects on learning. Cognitive Science. 1988;**12**(2):257-285

[4] Beatty J. Pupillometry: A psychophysiological approach. In: Psychophysiology: Systems, Processes, and Applications. Hillsdale, New Jersey: Erlbaum Associates; 1982. pp. 63-73

[5] Just MA, Carpenter PA. A theory of reading: From eye fixations to comprehension. Psychological Review. 1980;**87**(4):329-354

[6] Kok E, Jarodzka H. Before your Very Eyes: The Value and Limitations of Eye Tracking in Medical Education. The Association for the Study of Medical Education; 2017

[7] Lai ML et al. Eye tracking in educational research: A review. Educational Research Review. 2013;**10**:90-115

[8] Carter B, Luke S. Best practices in eye tracking research. International Journal of Psychophysiology. 2020;**155**:49-62

[9] Tatler BW, Wade NJ, Kwan H, Findlay JM, Velichkovsky BM. Yarbus, eye movements, and vision. i-Perception (SAGE Publications). 2010;**1**(1):7-27

[10] Ponce HR, Mayer RE, Loyola MS, Lopez M, Mendez EE. When two computer-supported learning strategies are better than one: An eye-tracking study. Computers and Education. 2018;**125**:376-388. DOI: 10.1016/j.compedu.2018.06.024

[11] Jacob RJ. The use of eye movements in human-computer interaction techniques: What you look at is what you get. ACM Transactions on Information Systems (TOIS). 1991;**9**(2):152-169

[12] Mashat A. An eye tracking study: What influences our visual attention on screens? In: Intelligent Computing: Proceedings of the 2019 Computing Conference. Vol. 2. London, United Kingdom: Springer International Publishing; 2019. pp. 1187-1192

[13] Alemdag E, Cagiltay K. Eye tracking in multimedia learning: A systematic review. Educational Research Review. 2018;**10**:90-115

[14] Poole A, Ball LJ. Eye tracking in HCI and usability research. In: Encyclopedia of Human Computer Interaction. Hershey, PA: IGI Global; 2006. pp. 211-219

[15] Liversedge SP, Findlay JM. Saccadic eye movements and cognition. Trends in Cognitive Sciences. 2000;**4**(1):6-14

[16] Enderson JM, Weeks PA Jr, Hollingworth A. The effects of semantic consistency on eye movements during complex scene viewing. Journal of Experimental Psychology: Human Perception and Performance. 1999;**25**(1):210

[17] Mele M, Federici S. A psychotechnological review on eye-tracking systems- towards user experience. Disability and Rehabilitation: Assistive Technology (London, UK). 2012;**7**(4):261-281

[18] McNamara DS, Jain A. Eye tracking in education: A review. Educational Psychology Review. 2019;**31**(1):1-28

Chapter 5

Standardising Scales for Arousal Metrics of Electrodermal Activity: A Case Study in Experience Design

Mati Mõttus, Marie-Laure Cazin and Pia Tikka

Abstract

In behavioural experiments, participants' experiences are usually measured on standardised scales, such as five-point Likert scales, which allow comparison of self-reported attitudes, affects, or other subjective experiences across individuals. Psychophysiological metrics, in turn, allow observation of bodily responses that can be indicators of unconscious decision-making, biases, or arousal, for example. The challenge is that physiological measurements require time-consuming steps of individual calibration before the data from different individuals can be compared with one another in a consistent manner. We argue the successful seamless standardisation during media experience could replace the lengthy prior calibration for each individual. We further assume that a few minutes of live data in the beginning of experience is enough to reliably map the data to a standard scale. This study used electrodermal activity (EDA) data, collected from 46 participants who were engaged in viewing a 19-minute long interactive virtual reality film. Six methods of data normalisation were compared upon two efficiency metrics. The results indicate Pareto scaling to be the most efficient method for standardising EDA arousal scales in real time. The reported novel method is expected to benefit the analysis of intersubjectively shared experiences in affective computing where arousal is designed to drive experiences with interactive media systems.

Keywords: user experience, physiological signals, electrodermal activity, implicit interactions, emotional arousal, data normalisation, affective computing

1. Introduction

Dictionary definition of standardisation refers to making something to conform to a measure, norm, or model in comparative evaluations. Standardisation of methods and procedures in the discipline of psychophysiology is one of the key issues to address in order to build a rigid basis for future advancements in the method developments, as well as for comparing the methods and findings from the new study designs with previous work [1], page 267. In this chapter, we will apply the idea of standardisation of procedures to a specific field of interactive media, where the participants' physiological responses are collected in real time during the media engagement, analysed, and then fed back to the media system so that the media system adapts to the input from the participants. While several physiological metrics allow tracking—and further describing—changes in the participants' emotional experiences when they are engaged in viewing or interacting with media content [1], we will focus on electrodermal activity (EDA).

Affective features of EDA are based on the skin's electrical conductance, which is related to the amount of sweat (moisture) in the skin. These features of EDA have repeatedly been shown to reliably indicate cognitive and affective modifications in human experience; see Ref. [2] for review. Affective features of EDA, for instance in the picture viewing paradigm, have been found related to emotional arousal; see for reference [1, 3] page 177. EDA signal has also been used in many pragmatic fields, such as polygraph [4]; workplace stress detection, e.g. Ref. [5]; and provision of health recommendations, e.g. Ref. [6]. In the field of arts, EDA has been used in interactive art installations to track the real-time user responses, e.g. see Ref. [7, 8].

Despite being well established, e.g. see Ref. [2], measuring EDA signal is not free of challenges. Three known problems with EDA are the signal noise, delay between stimulation and skin response, and individual differences in value range of the skin's electrical conductance measured in microsiemens (μS). While the EDA noise artefacts are sufficiently dealt with state-of-the-art signal filtering [9], the individual differences of value range and delays would require personal calibration before data collection. The amplitude of affective EDA responses may range individually between 0.1 and 5 μS [10]. Consequently, EDA-based measurement of arousal, unlike self-reported arousal, tends not to follow normal distribution nor fit standardised scales.

Here an example from the field of interactive cinema may concretise this problem. Our aim was to examine how to design user experience (UX) settings by controlling the film music in accordance with users' emotional arousal. In order to alter sequences of film music according to real-time measured arousal values, it is necessary to first measure the arousal before a sequence in order to replace the sequence with a suitable alternative. Making these measurements comparable across viewers, a rather lengthy personal calibration before the movie experience, is required. We believe that this calibration phase can be seamlessly completed during the first few minutes of the movie experience by standardising the scale of affective EDA response in real time.

Different mathematical methods of standardisation are available, but all of them require a full set of data being collected in order to calculate standardisation parameters, such as mean, standard deviation, minimum, maximum, or median. So these methods can actually be applied retrospectively, after the entire data from the session is collected, i.e. retrospective standardisation. The problem with data collection in real time is that calculations of real-time standardisation parameters can only use data from the beginning of a session up to the current moment of time. Towards the end of the data collection session, live and retrospective standardised values will be nearing each other and finally become equal (see **Figure 1** for an example). We assume live and retrospective standardisation results, calculated with different methods, will close up at different rates. The most suitable method would thus provide the fastest close-up rate to reach a predefined error margin (e.g. 5%) on the normalised scale.

The expected outcome is (1) to propose a most efficient algorithm for live standardisation of affective EDA response scale and (2) to provide insights on how to deploy this algorithm while designing media experiences that involve implicit real-time interactions with the media system. We are assuming artists or interaction designers to use the user-centred approach to design spectators' experiences according to their intentions. **Figure 2** illustrates how the expected outcome is meant to support

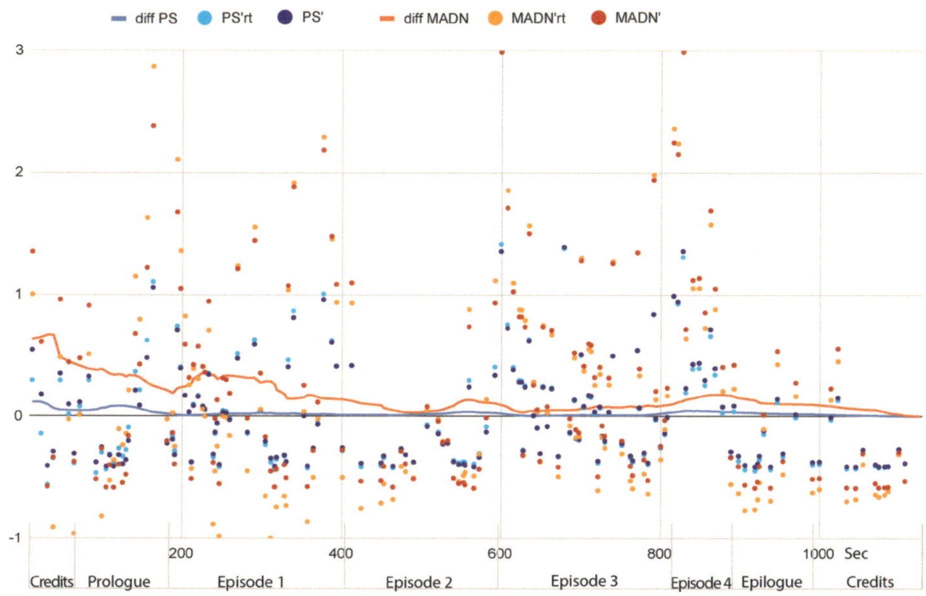

Figure 1.
Performance comparison of the worst (MADN) and the best (PS) methods during an example session of watching the movie. Red (MADN) and blue (PS) lines represent the changing difference between real-time and retrospective normalisation. Reddish and bluish dots represent SCR'_{RT} and SCR' of both methods. Movie episodes were added to the time axis for better comprehension.

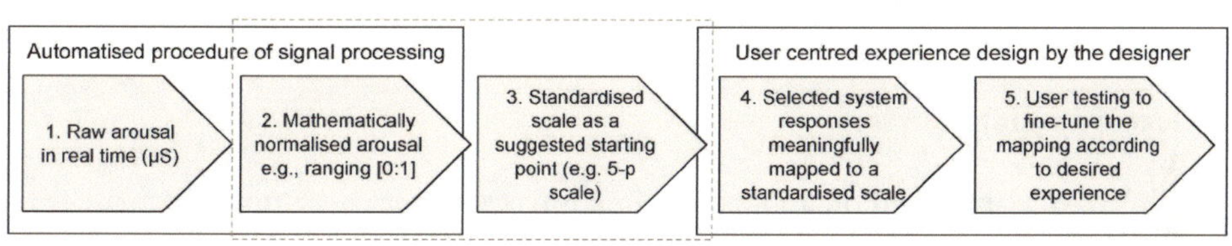

Figure 2.
Concept of data manipulations and design activities. Current chapter's focus is indicated with the dashed line.

the media artists in their workflow. Arousal data is used to drive implicit interactions with an interactive media. Using raw arousal data (1) requires individual calibration in order to map the arousal to the intended system response (4). The steps of mathematical normalisation (2) and suggested mapping of a standard scale (3) (dashed line box on **Figure 2**) are expected to provide a good starting point for user testing (5) to fine-tune the mappings (4). Steps 2 and 3 would later replace the individual calibration during the operation of an interactive system.

2. Theoretical background

2.1 Psychometric scales of emotional experience

Experiences characterised with emotional arousal during an interactive VR movie may be assessed in real time by tracking magnitudes of all momentary emotional responses throughout the film's timeline. Such magnitudes are known to be related to the values of affective features of EDA signal [1]. These values then can be used to calculate retrospectively the emotional experiences of the viewers during certain movie episodes of interest. Here, the assumption is that such experiences correspond to the mean of single, event-related responses of the same individual during a specific movie episode.

In their review, Mauss and Robinson [11] point out two approaches for measuring emotions. According to the dimensional approach, the emotions can be quantified by two dimensions: arousal and valence. The former describes magnitude and the latter polarity of the emotion; thus, the former corresponds to a normalised scale ranging [0,1], while the latter ranges [−1:1]. This theory simplifies understanding of emotions as the valence refers to the subjective feeling expressed on a good-bad, or positive-negative, scale. The other discrete emotion or basic emotion approach describes emotions with specific everyday words that people use for describing their emotional states, such as anger, sadness, or happiness. These two approaches of describing emotions are not necessarily contradicting, especially when evaluating the experience after a period of time where multiple different emotions may have occurred. Different discrete emotions may be retrospectively identified by the persons based on their own understanding on what these specific words mean for them but also in their shared cultural context. These words, for example, the experience of anger, can be regarded to overlap with the negative valence. In such a case, arousal appears to be an important measure in relation to both of these concepts as the film episodes can be described with discrete emotions (e.g. fear) or via emotional valence. During the design process, filmmakers rely on their previous experiences for predicting what type of valanced emotional responses the viewer could possibly experience when interacting with the film, or what type of discrete emotion words the viewer would retrospectively report having experienced.

2.2 Electrodermal activity

EDA metrics are based on an electrical manifestation of the sympathetic innervation of the skin's sweat glands [2]. Sweat glands are activated by the autonomic nervous system while not influenced by parasympathetic ("rest&digest"; "feed&breed") activity [12]. Certain features of skin conductance signal are known to be related to both mental and physical arousal, making them suitable to measure the amount of cognitive and physical, as well as emotional, activity [12, 13].

An EDA signal captures electrical conductance of the skin in time as shown in **Figure 3**. There are several features of EDA signal related to arousal. On one hand, the fluctuations of conductance in time, referred to as the phasic component of the signal, follow the emotional reactions to the encountered stimuli (**Figure 3**, blue line). On the other hand, the conductance also changes slowly, comprising the tonic component of the EDA signal, depicted as the red line in **Figure 3**.

The phasic peaks are here referred to as the skin conductance response (SCR), as suggested by Boucsein [13]. SCR is event related, describing reactions to certain stimuli. The peaks of phasic fluctuations correspond to the stimulus events where direct measures of emotional arousal are assumed to be the amplitudes of phasic peaks marked with "o" on **Figure 4**: the higher the peak amplitude, the stronger the emotional response to the stimulus [10].

Typical time-domain metrics of EDA signal are the number of SCR per time and the in-time average of SCR amplitude [9]. We assume these metrics could be used to describe arousal experience for that period. These metrics are derived from the phasic

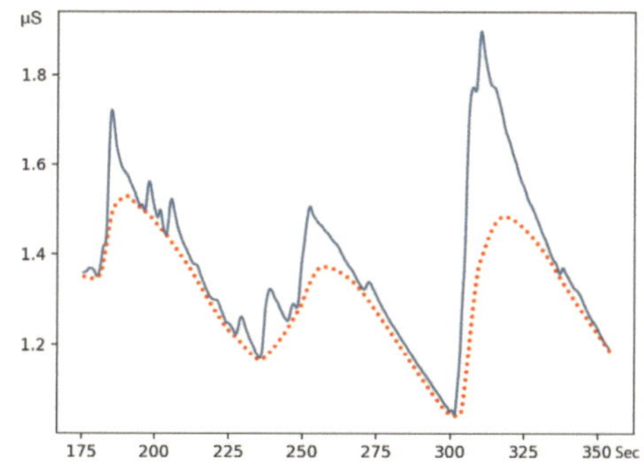

Figure 3.
Example of a typical raw EDA signal. A fragment was collected during the current study. Phasic component (blue) and tonic component (red).

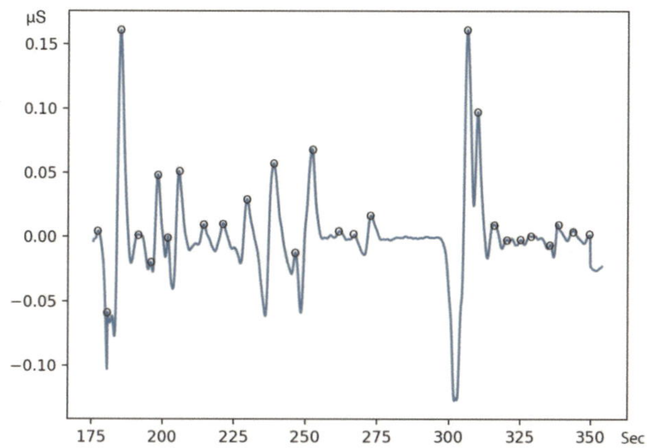

Figure 4.
An extracted phasic component of the signal in ***Figure 3****. Detected SCRs are marked with "o".*

component of EDA signal. The other time-domain metric, derived from the tonic component, follows the baseline of emotional arousal through a longer time period [1]. This baseline could also be used as an estimate of arousal in time: it drops during emotionally calm and rises during active periods (see the red line on **Figure 3**).

According to Leiner and Fahr [10], electrical properties of the skin and related SCR amplitudes vary across individuals from 0.01 to 5 μS. Electrical conductance of human skin ranges between 0.5 and 20 μS with rare exceptions [10, 13]. The individual variations stand for different base values of conductance as well as for different ranges where the conductance can change. In addition to that, skin reacts with delay, where the delays between stimulus events and corresponding SCR range across individuals from 1.5 to 6.5 seconds [10]. Therefore, the detection of stimulus-response causality appears uncertain if the gaps between consequent stimuli responses are less than 6.5 seconds. This is, audiovisual effects (e.g. showing a different image or playing a different sound) during an interactive film may be triggered in real time by individual SCR amplitudes of each viewer where these individual responses may also be delayed individually (from 1.5 to 6.5 seconds). Consequently, these effects will be both experienced differently and timed differently resulting in different experiences between different spectators.

2.3 Measuring emotions

The complex interdependence of emotions on both physiological and social factors has been outlined by social emotional theories, such as cognitive appraisal theory [14], network theories of emotion [15], and componential theories [16, 17]. In this work, we focused on the physiological dimensions of affective arousal, a phenomenon that has been shown to underlie reported emotional experiences, captured via EDA signal that can be measured with available tools. In what follows, our specific interest is in the formation of EDA signals, how the measured values can be inferred to indicate physiological responses related to emotional arousal, and furthermore, how these measures can be reliably conducted in real time during the participants' engagement with the interactive audio/visual media.

Suitability of a theory or a model for emotions in our context depended on two relevant aspects. First, its ability to explain the connection between physiological responses and emotional activity, and secondly, the ability to deal with temporal changes of participant's emotional responses due to the narrative-based structure of the movie. Component process model [18] provides three components, relevant in the current context: (1) cognitive appraisal, (2) physiological, and (3) subjective feeling. The notion of emotion is here defined according to the framework of component process model: "an episode of inter-related, synchronised changes in the states of all or most of the five organismic subsystems in response to the evaluation of an external or internal stimulus event as relevant to major concerns of the organism" [18]. This definition mentions the five organismic subsystems where physiological signals may originate, while adding the subjective feeling component (emotional experience) through an internal stimulus.

Mauss and Robinson [11] categorise measuring of emotions on one hand by data types being collected: (1) subjective self-reports, (2) objective physiological measurements, and (3) observations of behaviour. On the other hand, they differentiate between two ways of describing emotionality: discrete emotions (joy, fear, etc.) vs. dimensional (arousal-valence paradigm). Returning to the component process model [18], self-reports rely on cognitive appraisal and subjective feeling components, while physiological measurements are related to the physiological component. Self-reported data is normally collected on experiential psychometric scales: numeric, verbal, or pictorial rating scales, e.g. Likert scales in self-assessment manikin [19]. This data usually fits a more or less normal distribution and the scales are standardised. So the data can be reliably compared between individuals and between stimuli [11]. On one hand, SCR as an indicator of emotional arousal is directly related to the physiological component; on the other hand, the components of cognitive appraisal and subjective feeling in the component process model are known to be interrelated [18]. Thus, taking the quantitative nature of these components, where both cognitive appraisal and subjective feeling appear standardised in self-reports, in the work described here, we aim at proposing corresponding standardisation scale for the third component, physiological metrics of emotion.

2.4 Data normalisation and standardisation

Data normalisation is a common procedure in physiological computing [1]. Besides the term *normalisation*, referring to the results being normally distributed, the term *standardisation* has a special meaning for current study. It agrees with the call for disciplinary level of standardisation, e.g. see page 267 [1]; however, with the concept of standardisation, we refer to the work phase the examiner needs to conduct in order to be able to compare the real-time SCR values of one participant with the values of other participants, and additionally, mapping these values to the intended interactions with a media system. We refer to this point of decision-making as standardisation, because it requires an iterative user testing before the final conclusions of the process can be made: see the process model on **Figure 2**.

The current study understands the standardisation as a process of converting the physiometric numeric scales to match perceived feelings (e.g. emotional arousal) across individuals as closely as possible. In such a way, the feelings can be used to drive meaningful implicit interactions in cases where the same interactive system is used by different individuals. As discussed further in this chapter, unlike some of the mathematical normalisation methods, the standardisation process is expected to define the scales explicitly by providing start and endpoints as well as mapping rules (e.g. linear, logarithmic, or predefined).

The current work considers both signal processing and mathematical methods in data normalisation and standardisation. Individual calibration is a common practice to deal with individual peculiarities on signal processing level. This practice in the use of EDA is mentioned by Boucsein [13] and includes the exposure of conditioning stimuli before data collection to identify the calm base level of individual skin conductivity. Alternatively, the use of mathematical methods of normalisation is challenged by the fact that real-time data collection allows the data only up to the present moment of time. However, the mathematical methods, e.g. the ones reported by Singh and Singh [20], require a complete dataset (till the end of the movie) to proceed.

2.4.1 Signal processing

EDA signal processing includes various treatments to the raw signal where these treatments can significantly alter the detected value of arousal. In order to understand the treatments' effect on arousal value, the signal processing will be explained according to suggestions by Boucsein [13] and exemplified upon practical algorithms by Gabrieli et al. [9] and Aqajari et al. [21]. The latter work compared five signal processing algorithms in perspective of real-time emotion tracking.

Typical signal processing in affective EDA includes three steps: (1) noise reduction, (2) extraction of the phasic component, and (3) detecting phasic peaks and measuring their amplitudes. Signal processing algorithms use a number of parameters to proceed with these steps. In all steps, these parameters are suggested as a range. Step one, noise reduction, uses a bandpass filter with two parameters: lower and upper cut-off frequency (in Python code by Gabrieli et al. [9], the defaults respectively to 0.05 and 1 Hz). The low-pass filtering is suggested by Boucsein [13] at 0.1 or 1 Hz. Extraction of the phasic component uses a median filter in Gabrieli et al. [9] or mean filter in Aqajari et al. [21], with one parameter: the running time window (from 6 to 8 seconds). In step three, the phasic peaks are extracted as positive extremes of the phasic component. For example, the algorithm by Gabrieli et al. [9] assumes the peak onset happens at least 1 second after the stimulus event. However, this delay appears individual, varying from 1 to 3 seconds, suggested by Leiner [10] or from 1 to 4 seconds by Boucsein [13]. The effects of time and delay, mentioned in step three, may be handled by individual calibration for data normalisation; however, this has not been implemented in reviewed practical examples.

2.4.2 Mathematical methods

"Score normalisation refers to changing the location and scale parameters of the matching score distributions at the outputs of the individual matchers, so that the matching scores of different matchers are transformed into a common domain" [22]. Thirteen data normalisation methods were reviewed by Singh and Singh [20] with signal/data features' extraction perspective. The methods in comparison were divided into 6 distinct groups:

1. mean- and standard deviation–based normalisation (5);

2. minimum-maximum–based normalisation (2). These methods are "...highly sensitive to outliers in the data used for estimation, therefore it is not robust. The presence of outliers makes most of the data concentrate only in a smaller range" [22];

3. decimal scaling normalisation (1);

4. median and median absolute deviation normalisation (1). "...does not guarantee the common numerical range and is insensitive to outliers" [22];

5. tanh-based normalisation (2); and

6. sigmoidal normalisation (2).

These methods were evaluated by Singh and Singh [20] for classification accuracy of (a) feature selection and (b) feature weighting with typical machine learning algorithms, such as k-nearest neighbour learning, artificial neural networks, and support vector machines. The results indicated to avoid four methods: mean centred (MC), variable stability scaling (VSS), median absolute deviation normalisation (MADN), decimal scaling normalisation (DSN) in case the features do not vary logarithmically and recommended to use five methods: Z-score normalisation (ZSN), Pareto scaling (PS), min-max normalisation (MMN), tangential normalisation (TN), and sigmoidal normalisation (SN).

2.4.3 Efficiency of normalisation in affective EDA

How does data normalisation in machine learning (ML) relate to the current problem —real-time arousal tracking? Similar to the training of ML algorithms, real-time arousal tracking needs to consider personal peculiarities for reliable classification of arousal. Mathematical data normalisation methods require a full dataset to be applied; however, only the data up to the current moment of time of an individual is available in real-time data collection. For example, when mean- and standard deviation–based normalisation methods are used, means and standard deviations of full datasets are required to proceed. In real-time data collection, where the full dataset is not available, the means and standard deviations have to be predicted upon the data that has been collected so far. The more data gets collected, the closer real-time normalised values get to the retrospective values. We assume a real-time normalised SCR (SCR'_{RT}) will be nearing the retrospective normalised SCR (SCR') at different rates and times according to the normalisation method and characteristics of stimuli. We consider normalisation methods more efficient if they adapt to the standardised scale quicker during real-time data collection.

3. Method

3.1 Data

This study uses EDA data, collected from 46 participants during watching the VR 360 movie "Freud's last hypnosis" by Marie-Laure Cazin [23]. All sessions consisted of 8 emotionally distinct episodes: (1) opening credits about 1 minute; (2) prologue with a spoken narrative and minor visuals 2 minutes; (3–5) episodes with gradually increasing emotional tension, altogether about 11 minutes; (6) resolution with relaxing the tension; (7) concluding spoken narrative with minor visuals about 1:50 minutes; (8) end credits up to 2:40 minutes. The durations of sessions varied between 17:46 minutes and 19:04 minutes. Stimuli episodes are depicted over the time axis on **Figure 1**. EDA data was collected with NeuLog GSR sensors [24] through Unity game engine [25] with NeuLog API. SCRs were extracted and collected in order of occurrence with amplitudes and timestamps. The SCR peaks were calculated from raw EDA signals using PySiology package in Python [9].

In the current case study data, the range of electrical conductance of human skin appeared not as large as reported by earlier works [10, 13]. The recorded signals of a same person did not exceed the range of 2–5 μS. To avoid the effects of the response delay, we focused on averages over a 0.5–1-minute period of experience. This time window was considered because of the peculiarities of live signal processing: filtering for de-noising and extraction of the phasic component requires additional time to be completed. These considerations were based on recommendations for PySiology library of Python, used in the current study [9]. **Figures 3** and **4** were plotted using PySiology tools.

In the interactive film, the source of our EDA data, the calm prologue is followed by several episodes where tension builds up gradually towards the punchline and finally the relaxing epilogue. SCR data was processed with the parameters, suitable for driving the musical effects, relying on a number of these few-minute episodes of experience. The values of each episode were collected and mean values were used as marking the emotional experiences of the corresponding episodes, thus making the real-time standardisation context related.

3.2 Analysis

The aim of the analysis was to find the best method for standardising emotional arousal data during real-time emotion tracking. The "best" method is described as the fastest for SCR'_{RT} to reach and stay within the confidence bounds of SCR'. Python code by Gabrieli et al. [9] was used for signal processing. The original sample rate of the signal was 32 Hz, but it was downsampled to 10 Hz for further analysis to reduce computational load. Recommended values discussed in the Signal Processing subsection were used. SCR amplitudes were detected as the measure of emotional arousal for all participant sessions.

The following six normalisation methods were chosen for comparison based on discussions by Singh and Singh [20] and Latha and Thangasamy [22]:

1. min-max normalisation (MMN) brings values into the range [0,1]. The method is known to be sensitive to the outliers: $x'_n = (x_n - x_{min})/(x_{max} - x_{min})$;

2. Z-score normalisation (ZSN) brings values into the undefined bipolar range where the mean of x'n equals 0: $x'_n = (x_n - \mu)/\sigma$;

3. Pareto scaling (PS) brings values into the undefined bipolar range where the mean of x'n equals 0: $x'_n = (x_n - \mu)/\text{sqrt}(\sigma)$;

4. median absolute deviation normalisation (MADN) brings values into the undefined bipolar range where the median of x'n equals 0. The method is known to be insensitive to the outliers: $x'_n = (x_n - med_x)/med(|x_n - med_x|)$;

5. sigmoidal normalisation (SN) brings values into the range [0:1]. Suitable to the cases where logarithmic scales are preferred: $x'_n = 1/(1 + e - ^{q})$ where $q_n = (x_n - \mu)/\sigma$; and

6. decimal scaling normalisation (DSN) brings values into the range [0:1]. The method is known to be sensitive to the outliers: $x'_n = x_n/10^j$ where $j = \log_{10}(x_{max})$

Despite not being suggested by Singh and Singh [20], the MADN method was included in testing. The reason was that MADN is known to be insensitive to outliers. Additionally, unlike the other methods, it relies on medians and absolute deviations rather than means and standard deviations. Therefore, it was expected to produce a different distribution of values across the normalised scale, which might be beneficial in the current context.

3.2.1 Efficiency check

SCR'_{RT} results were calculated using the six methods above. Further idea was to compare these methods on how much time it takes for live standardisation scores to close up to the retrospective scores. The thresholds were pre-set to 0.05 for [0:1] scale and 0.1 for [−1:1] scale, corresponding to 5% of the scale length. The 30-second time window was used to evaluate the efficiency. The SCR' score in comparison was equal to the mean SCR' over 30-second period of experience. In such a way, the focus is on the respective movie experience but not on single emotional events. This approach is meant to avoid the effect of delays: skin response lag and additional time for signal processing. Besides efficiently coping with live standardisation, the methods were also compared for accuracy of data mapping. The stimulus—VR movie—was compiled to include all levels of emotional arousal. The entire standardised scale was expected to be used up with values distributed normally, peaking around the centre. Two known problems existed with tested normalisation methods: (1) sensitivity to outliers (MMN, DSN) and (2) undefined value range (ZSN, PS, MADN). If the normalisation method is sensitive to outliers, the distribution may appear skewed. Outliers can be understood as the few extreme values in a dataset. The presence of outliers makes most of the data concentrate only in a smaller range [22]. Insensitivity to outliers was assessed by comparing distributions of normalised data. Undefined value range was dealt with assessing whether the data distribution allows defining a reasonable scale in the current context. Ranking was completed subjectively by the authors via reviewing the histograms while considering the outliers.

4. Results

4.1 Efficiency of real-time normalisation

The methods in **Table 1** are ordered by performance, better ones first. Performance was classified upon mean time to reach and stay within the 5% level of

Method	Mean/ 95% (sec)	Min (sec)	Max (sec)
PS	171/60	13	891
MMN	281/76	13	1032
DSN	289/75	7	1032
SN	345/68	32	991
ZSN	675/65	108	1134
MADN	806/66	190	1087

Table 1.
All participants' average, minimum, and maximum times in seconds until the difference between SCR'RT and SCR' reaches and stays within 5% of the scale length.

difference between SCR'RT and SCR'—the mean duration of calibration phase. As can be seen from max times, better-performing methods were not always doing well. PS took more than 4 minutes to complete the calibration phase with 12 participants out of 46. The same failure for the second-performing method (MMN) and the third (DSN) was respectively with 13 and 19 participants.

4.2 Outliers and defined scale range

All three best-performing methods in **Table 1** were affected by outliers. Additionally, the best one (PS) did not bring values to defined range. The histograms, used to evaluate the methods, are depicted in **Figure 5**. The histograms use predefined scales with ranges [0:1] for SN, MMN, and DSN and [−1:1] for PS, MADN, and ZSN. The ranges were predefined by authors based on study data. The histograms of MMN and DSN show clearly a skewed distribution, but PS looks promising with trending values around halfway of the scale. The data revealed 1.1% of SCR' values by PS were greater than the predefined range. These 1.1% were considered as rare outliers to be mapped using some other rules, which will be discussed later. The data also revealed that none of the SCR' values by PS appeared smaller than −0.5, which may suggest cutting the scale at −0.5. **Table 2** shows how many of the SCR' values by all methods exceeded the histogram ranges.

5. Discussion

To understand better, what method to use, we compared the following methods: ZSN, PS, MMN, DSN, MADN, and SN The results of method comparison show that PS does perform best in coping with real-time calibration. PS is also promising in perspective of mapping the data so that the resulting scale really appears well standardised, for example designing musical effects for a VR movie through implicit interactions. The following discussion handles two main issues of designing implicit interactions meaningfully: (1) how to handle the delays in SCR detection? and (2) how to distribute the values across the scale? Meaningfulness of implicit interactions depends on specific goals of an interactive artist. We assume experience design principles [26] with user-centred approach [27] to be deployed by interactive artists. User-centred design approach requires the piece of art to undergo testing with users (spectators and experiencers) in order to fine-tune its features before being publicly shown.

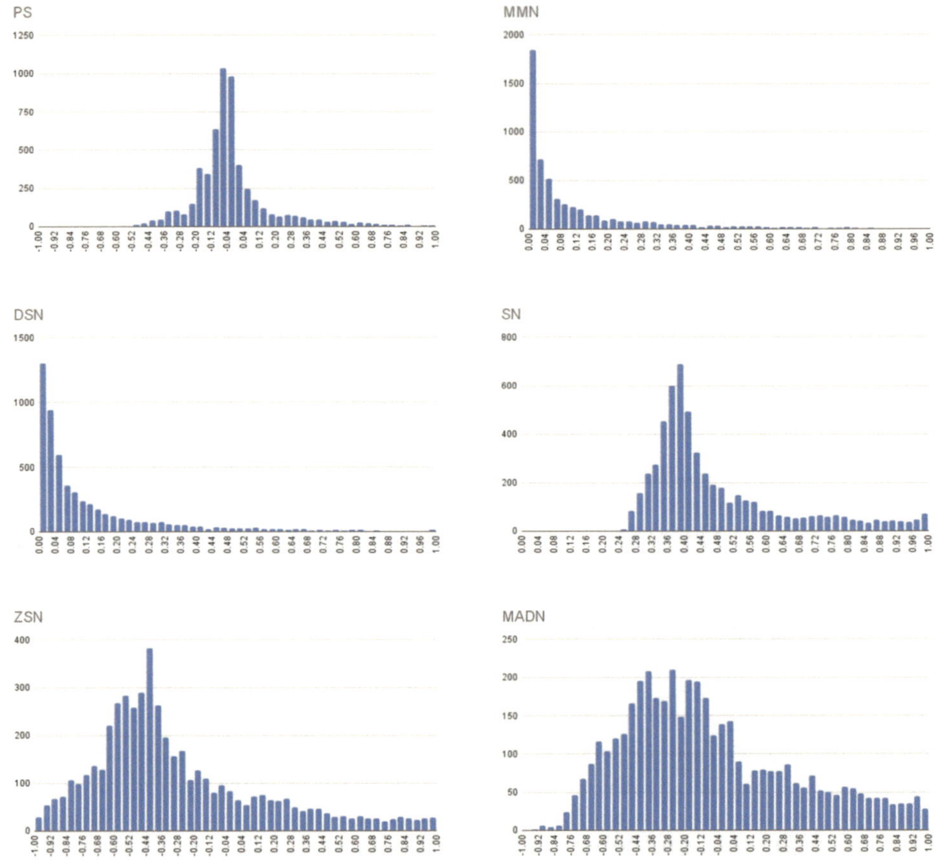

Figure 5.
Distribution of normalised results.

data [x:y]	ZSN	PS	MMN	SN	MADN	DSN
>y	672(12%)	60(11%)	0	0	1332(24%)	0
<x	41(0.7%)	0	0	0	0	0
Total SCR	5627	5627	5627	5627	5627	5627

Table 2.
SCR' count and (%) outside the predefined histogram ranges.

The idea of experience design, in turn, is about meaningfully inducing spectators' certain experiences through design. For example, in an interactive media, the music can be used to either reduce or enforce the emotional experience of thrill or calmness, alternatively. In either of the cases, making a suitable choice is a matter of experience design, where the choice is justified through testing. Such testing allows the artist to shape spectators' experiences with a purpose. Whatever the purpose, experiential scales when standardised across experiencers would provide a good starting point to prepare a prototype for user testing. The following discussion aims to explain reasons behind such a starting point by first providing a context-related example.

5.1 Comparison of best- and worst-performing methods in current context

Figure 1 represents the performance of two methods during an example session. The best- and worst-performing methods were compared to illustrate how the efficiency was evaluated. The example session was chosen where the best-performing method did quite well, while the other method never performed well. The difference between SCR'_{RT} and SCR' is closing up zero by the end of the session, where the real-time and retrospective SCR' scores are equal. The 5% threshold was set to 0.1 for both methods, assuming a meaningful range of scales for both methods [−1:1]. Efficiency was evaluated as the time where the threshold was reached and held (calibration phase completed). In this example, PS reaches the threshold in 30 seconds and MADN in 991 seconds. **Figure 1** also illustrates outliers. Outliers appear as scores that deviate significantly from mainstream's range. Our rationale behind predefining the range of [−1:1] was based on how the outliers were spread. In this example, the real range stretched from −0.56 to 1.41 (PS) and from −2.51 to 3.27 (MADN), while the mainstream scores, according to histograms (**Figure 5**), fit the range [−1:1] more (PS) or less (MADN).

5.2 Timing of implicit interactions

The timeline of relevant movie episodes was added in **Figure 1** to illustrate the emotional experience during the VR movie. This example reflects a single individual; however, there were common trends across the participants. One of these was the excitement caused by the VR environment, which made the intentionally calm episodes more aroused in the beginning of the movie (start credits and prologue), compared to the similar episodes in the end (epilogue and end credits). During the first episode, this excitement gradually faded and spectators became more focused on the narrative for the rest of the movie. Real-time values of PS ("PS'_{RT}" on **Figure 1**) should sufficiently fit standard scale by the beginning of the first episode (171 ± 60 sec in average to complete the calibration phase), so the SCR-based implicit interactions can be safely started in the beginning of the first episode.

The other issue besides the reasonable starting point of implicit interactions is the length of experience episode. To mitigate the effect of delays in SCR detection, a 30-second time window was used while establishing the most efficient normalisation method. This is why at least 30-second experience is recommended to drive the implicit interactions. The study data shows an average participant had 122 SCR during the movie. This makes an average 30-second window contain 3.33 SCR. In many occasions, only one SCR occurred in 30 seconds, and in a few occasions, none occurred. Therefore, the authors suggest further testing with a 40–60-second time window. The interactions will still be smooth in time, as the window slides through the timeline along with the playhead.

5.3 Scale mapping

SCR-based implicit interactions make sense upon meaningful interpretation of arousal. Depending on the nature of a desired system response (a musical effect), the arousal can be mapped on either a continuous or stepped scale. Continuous scales support smoothly controlling the sound parameters, such as volume or timbre, while stepped scale allows switching between alternative samples or instruments.

Besides the two common mapping algorithms for continuous scale—linear and logarithmic—any other mathematical rules can be used for meaningful interactions. Logarithmic scales make sense, for example, in cases when the musical effect needs to be more substantial for higher arousal levels while remaining marginal between medium and low levels.

For stepped scales, the number of steps in a scale should correspond to the number of alternative system responses. For example with two alternatives, the scale mapping is defined by one threshold value, and three alternatives require defining two thresholds, etc. Mapping a stepped scale means defining the thresholds. An advantage of the stepped scale is when the number of steps is lower the real-time calibration becomes less strict: instead of 5% tolerance in the example on **Figure 1**, the 10% or even 20% tolerance could be sufficient. For example, the film music can be interactively modified by adding distinct instruments to the initial orchestra — the melodic piano when low, but sharp drums when high arousals are detected — otherwise no additional instruments were added. In this case, the whole scale is divided into three arousal levels—low, medium, and high—requiring less tolerance than dividing it into five or seven.

For a good starting point, either with continuous or stepped scales, the authors suggest to cut the bottom range at −0.5. Special mapping rules may be useful to distinguish arousal levels that occur most often. According to **Figure 1**, the individual SCR' values of PS can often jump to extremes of the range [−0.5:1.4]. The time window–based average, suggested by the shape of the histogram, probably does not fluctuate as much. The histogram of PS indicates 78% of SCR values fall within [−0.2:0.2], suggesting focusing on this range as a good starting point. For example, in case of a stepped scale, the values outside this range can be classified accordingly as "low" (<−0.2) or "high" (>0.2), while the values within the range may be divided into three (e.g. "medium low", "medium", and "medium high") or more steps. For a continuous scale, the increment of scale may be set dependent on the steepness of the histogram curve: the higher the steepness, the smaller the increment. For example, within [−0.2:0.2], the increment is substantially smaller than outside that range. After using the suggested starting point for user testing, smaller corrections of mapping are expected based on test results to fine-tune the interactive system.

5.4 Conditions of using the proposed starting point in user experience design

The current case was about EDA-based emotional arousal values. SCR amplitudes of EDA signal were used to interpret the value of arousal. The best suitable normalisation method and scale mapping ideas, proposed earlier in discussion, may not apply for other emotion-related physiological signals or the other features of EDA. We expect further studies to address these other cases.

As already stated earlier, emotion-related physiological responses tend to be personal. The outcome of the study aims for seamless personal calibration, this is, the experiencer is not supposed to notice the calibration phase while having an interactive (e.g. media) experience. Based on our findings, interaction designers could consider possible durations of calibration phases when designing meaningful implicit interactions in order to provide personalised UX. Diversity in UX originates from four sources—*individual* as the user, *product* as an interactive system, *situation*, and *time* [28]. The following part of the discussion addresses strengths and weaknesses of the proposed approach in these four perspectives.

5.4.1 Individual

Interactive movies are meant for different viewers and the same individuals usually watch the same film once. Here, the re-calibration of the system is essential for each participant session. EDA can also be deployed in a variety of applications of personal devices such as smartphones and -watches, mainly used solely by the owner. In these cases, EDA-based arousal scales need to be calibrated once with an option to re-calibrate from time to time. If the calibration happens seamlessly, and it reaches the desired tolerance threshold, it may not be repeated unless the owner is changed or specifically requested by the current owner.

5.4.2 Product

Interactive systems can be categorised based on the purpose as pragmatic and leisure related. The former is more related to pragmatic, and latter to hedonic experiences. Emotional arousal plays a role in both the categories, though the current case was about interactive media for leisure. The outcome is therefore more suitable for leisure (e.g. art, games, and media) while requiring extra caution in pragmatic solutions, where the overall emotionality tends to be lower. Seamless calibration relies on the data sample from the seamless calibration phase, adapting the standardised scale to the parameters of that sample. Pareto scaling, for example, relies on mean and standard deviation of that data sample to produce the standardised values. When the scale is adapted to low mean and standard deviation of calibration phase, the higher SCR amplitudes, further into the session, would not fit to the standardised arousal scale, thus resulting in misinterpretation of the arousal value. The proposed method should not be used in evaluation tools (e.g. evaluating emotional experience in UX research) or safety critical systems, such as in medicine or transportation. However, the proposed method could be used in systems where arousal tracking supports some other methods, for example in mitigating stress or fatigue where the main method is video observation.

5.4.3 Situation

The current data was collected in a VR environment where the viewer is isolated from surroundings by the VR headset, though most daily interactions with technology happen in environments that are full of emotional stimuli. If deployed in such interactive systems, the outer stimuli will definitely have an effect on seamless calibration. Awareness of the real situation causing an emotional reaction while being immersed in VR movie experience was reported several times by the participants of the current study. It is possible that an alternative normalisation method (other than Pareto scaling) appears more efficient for seamless calibration in situations with strong outer emotional stimuli and situations where the user is wearing a VR headset that frames the experiential event space by technological means of altered audio-visual 3D space.

5.4.4 Time

The proposed starting point for scale mapping is about a few-minute period in the beginning of the experience, which determines how time matters. Firstly, the approach is suitable when the whole experience is long enough to allow such a few-minute calibration phase. The calibration phase can actually continue throughout the whole experience, gradually improving the standard mapping of arousal. Secondly, the seamless standardisation will be more reliable when the emotional experience is consistent in time, i.e. the experience in the beginning is not too different from the experience later in the session. If these cases do not apply, a special non-seamless calibration episode may be required.

6. Conclusion

This study proposes to use the Pareto scaling method for standardising the SCR-driven arousal scales in real time. Real-time standardisation is a seamless process that is expected to replace personal calibration of EDA-based interactive systems. As an additional outcome, we propose a good starting point for user testing. The starting point suggests two relevant estimates to begin with: firstly, the duration of the time window for measuring real-time experience in order to mitigate the effect of delays of skin reaction and secondly, the rules for mapping of arousal scales in relation to the nature of desired interactions. The results of the study are limited to implicit interactions where the reliability is not critical, such as interactive art. Safety-critical systems, such as health and well-being equipment, as well as high-credibility tools, such as polygraph, should still be used by experts with personal calibration. The study data was collected during VR movie experiences, but we assume the same recommendations could be used for designing other kinds of interactive art experiences, such as music, painting, theatre, or dance performance. We expect further studies to prove or reject this assumption as well as come up with additional context-related recommendations for each field of application.

Acknowledgements

The work has been supported by EU Mobilitas Plus Top Researcher Grant (MOBTT90) and Team Grant (PRG2109) awarded for P. Tikka and EU Mobilats Pluss Postdoc grant awarded for M.-L. Cazin, funded by the Estonian Research Council and LS2N Laboratory, Nantes University, France.

Abbreviations

EDA	electrodermal activity
SCR	skin conductance response
MADN	median absolute deviation normalisation
DSN	decimal scaling normalisation
ZSN	Z-score normalisation
PS	pareto scaling
MMN	minimum-maximum normalisation
SN	sigmoidal normalisation

Author details

Mati Mõttus[1*], Marie-Laure Cazin[2] and Pia Tikka[3]

1 Tallinn University, School of Digital Technologies, Tallinn, Estonia

2 Ecole Supérieure d'Art et de Design -TALM Le Mans, France

3 Tallinn University, Baltic Film, Media and Arts School, Tallinn, Estonia

*Address all correspondence to: matim@tlu.ee

References

[1] Cowley B, Filetti M, Lukander K, Torniainen J, Henelius A, Ahonen L, et al. The psychophysiology primer: A guide to methods and a broad review with a focus on human–computer interaction. Foundations and Trends in Human-Computer Interaction. 2015;**9** (3–4):151-308. DOI: 10.1561/1100000065

[2] Posada-Quintero HF, Chon KH. Innovations in electrodermal activity data collection and signal processing: A systematic review. Sensors (Basel, Switzerland). 2020;**20**(2):479. DOI: 10.3390/s20020479

[3] Lang PJ, Greenwald MK, Bradley MM, Hamm AO. Looking at pictures: Affective, facial, visceral, and behavioral reactions. Psychophysiology. 1993;**30**(3):261-273

[4] Rosenfeld JP. Alternative views of Bashore and Rapp's (1993) alternatives to traditional polygraphy: A critique. Psychological Bulletin. 1995;**117**:159-166. DOI: 10.1037/0033-2909.117.1.159

[5] Setz C, Arnrich B, Schumm J, La Marca R, Tröster G, Ehlert U. Discriminating stress from cognitive load using a wearable EDA device. IEEE Transactions on Information Technology in Biomedicine. 2010;**14**(2):410-417. DOI: 10.1109/TITB.2009.2036164

[6] Regalia G, Onorati F, Lai M, Caborni C, Picard RW. Multi-modal wrist-worn devices for seizure detection and advancing research: Focus on the empatica wristbands. Epilepsy Research. 2019;**153**:79-82. DOI: 10.1016/j.eplepsyres.2019.02.007

[7] Tikka P, Vuori R, Kaipainen M. Narrative logic of enactive cinema: Obsession. Digital Creativity. 2006;**17**(4):205-212. DOI: 10.1080/14626260601074078

[8] Sugawa M, Furukawa T, Chernyshov G, Hynds D, Han J, Padovani M, et al. Boiling mind: Amplifying the audience-performer connection through Sonification and visualization of heart and electrodermal activities. In: Proceedings of the Fifteenth International Conference on Tangible, Embedded, and Embodied Interaction (TEI'21). New York, NY, USA: Association for Computing Machinery; 2021. pp. 1-10

[9] Gabrieli G, Azhari A, Esposito G. PySiology: A python package for physiological feature extraction. In: Esposito A, Faundez-Zanuy M, Morabito F, Pasero E, editors. Neural Approaches to Dynamics of Signal Exchanges. Smart Innovation, Systems and Technologies. Vol. 151. Singapore: Springer; 2020

[10] Leiner DJ, Fahr A, Früh H. EDA positive change: A simple algorithm for electrodermal activity to measure general audience arousal during media exposure. Communication Methods and Measures. 2012;**6**(4):237-250. DOI: 10.1080/19312458.2012.732627

[11] Mauss IB, Robinson MD. Measures of emotion: A review. Cognition and Emotion. 2009;**23**(2):209-237. DOI: 10.1080/02699930802204677

[12] Dawson ME, Schell AM, Filion DL. The electrodermal system. In: Cacioppo JT, Tassinary LG, Berntson GG, editors. Handbook of Psychophysiology. Cambridge Handbooks in Psychology. Cambridge, UK: Cambridge University Press; 2016. pp. 217-243

[13] Boucsein W. Electrodermal Activity. New York, NY: Springer Science &

Business Media, Springer; 2012. DOI: 10.1007/978-1-4614-1126-0

[14] Lazarus RS. Emotion and Adaptation. Oxford, UK: Oxford University Press; 1991

[15] Lang PJ. The varieties of emotional experience: A meditation on James–Lange theory. Psychological Review. 1994;**101**(2):211-221. PubMed: 8022956

[16] Frijda NH. The Emotions. Cambridge: Cambridge University Press; 1986

[17] Frijda NH. Emotion, cognitive structure, and action tendency. Cognition and Emotion. 1987;**1**:115-143

[18] Scherer R. What are emotions? And how can they be measured? Social Science Information. 2005;**44**(4): 695-729

[19] Bradley MM, Lang PJ. Measuring emotion: The self-assessment manikin and the semantic differential. Journal of Behavior Therapy and Experimental Psychiatry. 1994;**25**(1):49-59, ISSN 0005-7916

[20] Singh D, Singh B. Investigating the impact of data normalization on classification performance. Applied Soft Computing. 2020;**97**(Part B):105524. ISSN 1568-4946. DOI: 10.1016/j.asoc.2019.105524

[21] Aqajari SAH, Naeini EK, Mehrabadi MA, Labbaf S, Dutt N, Rahmani AM. pyEDA: An open-source python toolkit for pre-processing and feature extraction of electrodermal activity. Procedia Computer Science. 2021;**184**:99-106

[22] Latha L, Thangasamy S. Efficient approach to normalization of multimodal biometric scores. International Journal of Computer Applications. 2011;**32**(10):57-64

[23] Vigier T, Cazin M-L. Demo Emotive VR: A Neuro-Interactive 360 Movie (Version 1). TVX2018, ACM Conference Demo, Figshare. 2018. DOI: 10.6084/m9.figshare.6527462.v1

[24] GSR Logger Sensor NUL-217, Specifications. NeuLog Logger Sensors. Available from: https://neulog.com/gsr/#sensorguide [Accessed: September 12, 2024]

[25] Unity Manual, Video and Cutscenes. Unity Technologies. Available from: https://docs.unity3d.com/Manual/Video.html [Accessed: September 12, 2024]

[26] Hassenzahl M. Experience Design: Technology for all the Right Reasons, Synthesis Lectures on Human-Centered Informatics. Switzerland AG: Springer Nature; 2010. ISSN 1946-7680

[27] Norman DA, Draper SW. User Centered System Design. New Perspectives on Human-Computer Interactio. USA: L. Erlbaum Associates Inc; 1986. ISBN: 978-0-89859-781-3

[28] Karapanos E. Quantifying diversity in user experience [unpublished PhD thesis]. Eindhoven, Netherlands: Eindhoven University of Technology; 2010

Chapter 6

The Best and Most Efficient Video Compression Methods

Yaghoub Saberi, Mohammadreza Forghani and Sharifeh S. Mirkhalaf

Abstract

In today's digital era, video compression stands as a crucial element in managing and transmitting multimedia data efficiently. This chapter offers a comprehensive examination and analysis of various video compression techniques, aiming to identify and compare methods based on their effectiveness and efficiency. This chapter begins by exploring classic algorithms such as discrete cosine transform (DCT) and Huffman coding, then transitions to an in-depth analysis of modern standards, including H.264/AVC, H.265/HEVC, and H.266/VVC. It assesses the impact of these methods on image quality, storage requirements, and computational complexity. Additionally, the chapter delves into recent advancements in utilizing artificial intelligence and deep learning to enhance video compression performance and presents innovative techniques in this field. The primary objective of this chapter is to provide practical guidance for selecting the most suitable compression method based on specific user needs and various application scenarios.

Keywords: video compression, compression algorithms, HEVC, VVC, artificial intelligence

1. Introduction

In today's world, videos play an irreplaceable role in information transfer, entertainment, and communication. Video compression is a process that reduces the size of video data, enabling faster transmission and more efficient storage. This technique significantly decreases the volume of video data while maintaining acceptable quality, which is crucial in the multimedia world. Given the growing production of videos and the need for their transmission and storage across limited networks and various devices, video compression has become a key technology. The importance of video compression lies in its role in supporting a range of multimedia applications. From live streaming of sports events and television programs to sharing personal videos on social media, video compression reduces data volume and enhances efficiency in transmission and storage [1]. Additionally, this technology holds special significance in applications such as video conferencing, video games, and online streaming. With significant advancements in video compression algorithms, new and efficient standards such as H.265/high efficiency video Coding (HEVC), VP9, AOMedia Video

1 (AV1), and recently versatile video coding (VVC) have been introduced. These standards utilize advanced and optimized techniques to enable higher-quality video compression with lower bitrates. This chapter will explore the best and most efficient video compression methods. It will first review the fundamental concepts and principles of video compression and then introduce and analyze advanced compression algorithms. Finally, the chapter will examine the applications of these algorithms in the industry and the future challenges for video compression. This comprehensive review will aid in a better understanding of the advantages, disadvantages, and future of video compression technology [2].

2. Basic concepts of video compression

The following provides explanations of concepts and terminology used in video compression. These explanations will give you a comprehensive understanding of the fundamental concepts of video compression and related key terms, which are essential for grasping more advanced topics.

2.1 Principles of compression

Data compression is a method used to minimize the size of digital data, particularly in multimedia applications like video. The primary goal of compression is to reduce the volume of data while preserving acceptable quality. This allows for faster transmission over bandwidth-constrained networks and more efficient storage on devices with limited capacities. Compression is widely applied in various video-related applications, such as online streaming, video conferencing, and video transmission over the Internet. The process of video compression consists of several sequential stages aimed at reducing the data volume. First, the video data is analyzed to detect redundant or less significant information. Redundancies are then minimized by techniques such as motion prediction, which removes similar sections across different frames. Following this, the remaining data is encoded using specific compression algorithms, reducing both storage requirements and bandwidth consumption [3].

Several key techniques are employed to achieve video compression, each playing an essential role in reducing data size. Inter-frame and intra-frame encoding are the primary methods used in combination. Inter-frame encoding reduces redundant information between adjacent frames by utilizing data from neighboring frames, while intra-frame encoding compresses each frame independently. Motion prediction further optimizes the process by predicting object movement across consecutive frames, allowing only changes to be stored. Additionally, quantization converts continuous data into discrete values to further decrease data size, although this step can lead to some loss of detail and is typically part of lossy compression methods [4].

2.2 Difference between lossy and lossless compression

Lossless compression is a technique where all the original video data is fully preserved, meaning no information is lost during the compression process. This method works by removing redundancies in the data, allowing the compressed video to be decompressed back to its exact original form. Lossless compression is ideal for situations where maintaining the highest possible quality is critical, such as in the archiving of high-quality videos or the storage of scientific data. However, it has limited effectiveness in reducing file sizes compared to lossy compression, as it retains more data. In contrast, lossy compression reduces file size by removing video information considered less important, such as minor details or subtle variations in color and brightness. This method significantly decreases video size by compromising some quality, though the loss is often imperceptible to the human eye. Lossy compression is ideal for scenarios where file size and transmission speed are prioritized over perfect image quality, such as in online video streaming, where smaller file sizes enable quicker downloads and less bandwidth usage. The choice between lossless and lossy compression depends largely on the application. Lossless compression is typically used in contexts where maintaining the original video quality is essential, such as in medical imaging, educational videos, or scientific recordings. On the other hand, lossy compression is more commonly used in applications where reducing file size and transmission speed are more important, such as in streaming platforms, social media, and entertainment video storage [5].

2.3 Key terms and concepts

Frame rate: Frame rate refers to the number of frames displayed per second of video. This metric has a significant impact on the smoothness of motion and transitions in the video. A higher frame rate (e.g., 60 frames per second) results in smoother and more natural movement, while a lower frame rate (e.g., 24 or 30 frames per second) can lead to choppy or unnatural motion. The choice of frame rate depends on the type of content and video application; for instance, higher frame rates are preferred in video games or sports videos, while 24 frames per second is typically used in cinematic films [6].

Resolution: Resolution refers to the number of pixels in each frame of the video, usually expressed as the number of horizontal pixels by vertical pixels (e.g., 1920 x 1080 for Full HD). Higher resolution means more detail and better image quality, but it requires more data and bandwidth for transmission. Common resolutions include HD (720p), Full HD (1080p), 4 K (2160p), and more recently 8 K (4320p). The choice of resolution depends on the content type, display device, and user requirements [7].

Bitrate: Bitrate refers to the amount of data transferred or stored per second of video and has a direct impact on video image quality. Higher bitrate implies better image quality but requires more bandwidth and storage space. Bitrate can be applied in two modes: constant bitrate (CBR) and variable bitrate (VBR). In CBR mode, the bitrate remains constant throughout the video, resulting in consistent image quality, making it suitable for live streaming and video playback. In contrast, VBR mode adjusts the bitrate according to the video content; it increases during complex scenes and decreases during simpler ones, leading to higher quality and reduced data size, making it suitable for high-quality video storage [8].

3. Video compression algorithms

Video compression is used to reduce the size of video data and optimize its transmission and storage. This section examines the fundamental algorithms used in video compression.

3.1 Basic compression algorithms

Basic compression algorithms are fundamental and effective methods used to reduce data size, often forming the initial steps in video compression. These algorithms include:

Run-length encoding (RLE) is one of the simplest forms of data compression. It works by reducing the size of data that contains repeated elements. RLE identifies long sequences of the same value and replaces them with a pair representing the value and its count. For instance, the sequence "AAAAABBBCCDAA" is compressed into "5A3B2C1D2A." This method is particularly effective for compressing graphic images with repetitive pixels, such as black-and-white images. However, it is less effective when dealing with highly variable data, where the compression gain is minimal. Huffman coding is another widely used lossless compression technique that relies on frequency-based encoding. In this algorithm, the most frequent characters are encoded using shorter binary strings, while less frequent characters are represented by longer strings. For example, if the letter "E" occurs frequently in a text, it might be encoded as "0," while a less common letter would be assigned a longer binary sequence. Huffman coding is highly efficient for compressing text and images and forms the backbone of compression formats like Joint Photographic Experts Group (JPEG) and portable network graphics (PNG), thanks to its optimal variable-length encoding based on a tree structure [9].

Discrete cosine transform (DCT) is a critical algorithm for image and video compression, providing the foundation for widely used standards like JPEG, Motion Picture Experts Group (MPEG), and H.264. DCT transforms input data from the time or spatial domain into the frequency domain, enabling the separation of different frequency components. In video and image data, the most important details are concentrated in lower frequencies, while higher frequencies usually contain less critical information and noise. DCT focuses on compressing the lower frequencies and reducing or eliminating the higher ones, significantly decreasing data size. While DCT introduces some loss of image quality, the loss is typically minimal and imperceptible in most applications. These foundational algorithms serve as the basis for more complex video compression systems, and when combined with advanced methods, they enable substantial reductions in data size without significantly compromising quality [10].

3.2 Advanced compression algorithms

Advanced video compression algorithms play a crucial role in reducing video data size and improving transmission and storage efficiency. These algorithms, utilizing sophisticated and optimized techniques, have introduced new standards that have revolutionized the multimedia industry. This section provides a more detailed examination of these standards.

3.2.1 MPEG (motion picture experts group)

The MPEG has been a pioneer in developing video compression standards since the 1980s, providing widely accepted standards for audio and video compression. MPEG-1, introduced in 1993, was designed to compress video home system (VHS)-quality video and audio CDs, enabling digital compression for home videos and CDs. MPEG-2, introduced in 1995, became one of the most commonly used standards for digital TV broadcasting and DVDs, providing high-quality video compression and quickly becoming adopted in digital TV broadcasting. MPEG-4, introduced in 1999, brought significant advances by offering tools for compressing high-definition videos and transmitting multimedia data over low-bandwidth networks. Its AVC/H.264 profile is extensively used in online video streaming and video data storage. MPEG-H, which includes advanced technologies such as high efficiency video coding (HEVC), introduced in 2013 for compressing 4 K and 8 K videos, provides very high efficiency and excellent image quality using more sophisticated motion prediction and inter- or intra-frame encoding techniques [11].

3.2.2 VP9 (introduced in 2013)

VP9 is a video compression algorithm developed by Google and introduced in 2013 as a successor to VP8. This algorithm is specifically designed for streaming video on online services like YouTube and aims to reduce bitrates while maintaining high quality. VP9 utilizes advanced techniques such as inter- and intra-frame coding, adaptive quantization, and complex motion prediction models. One of VP9's notable features is its ability to reduce bitrate by up to 50% compared to H.264/AVC without noticeable quality loss. This feature has made VP9 a popular standard for streaming high-definition (HD and 4 K) videos and for videos that require low bandwidth [12].

3.2.3 AV1 (introduced in 2018)

AV1, or AOMedia Video 1, is a video compression standard developed by the Alliance for Open Media (AOMedia) and introduced in 2018. Designed as a strong competitor to H.265/HEVC and a successor to VP9, AV1 has quickly gained traction in the industry due to its superior bitrate reduction capabilities without quality degradation. AV1 employs advanced techniques such as adaptive frame partitioning, complex inter- and intra-frame coding, and machine learning-based optimizations. This standard is especially effective in streaming 4 K and high dynamic range (HDR) videos, where high performance and quality without degradation are crucial. AV1 can reduce bitrate by up to 30% more than VP9 and 50% more than H.264/AVC, making it one of the preferred standards for very high-resolution video streaming and low-bandwidth applications [13].

3.2.4 H.264/AVC (introduced in 2003)

H.264/advanced video coding (AVC) is one of the most widely used video compression standards, jointly developed in 2003 by ITU-T Video Coding Experts Group (VCEG) and ISO/IEC Moving Picture Experts Group (MPEG). Also known as MPEG-4 Part 10, this standard was quickly adopted across various industries due to its excellent balance between image quality and compression efficiency. H.264/AVC significantly reduces the bitrate required to maintain high image quality using advanced techniques such as inter- and intra-frame coding, adaptive quantization, and optimized motion prediction. A key feature of H.264/AVC is its use of advanced motion prediction methods. These standards employ smaller blocks (as small as 4 x 4 pixels) for motion analysis, providing higher accuracy in motion prediction and reducing redundancy between frames. This technique, along with the use of multiple reference frames, allows H.264/AVC to reduce bitrate by up to 50% compared to previous standards like MPEG-2, while significantly improving image quality [14].

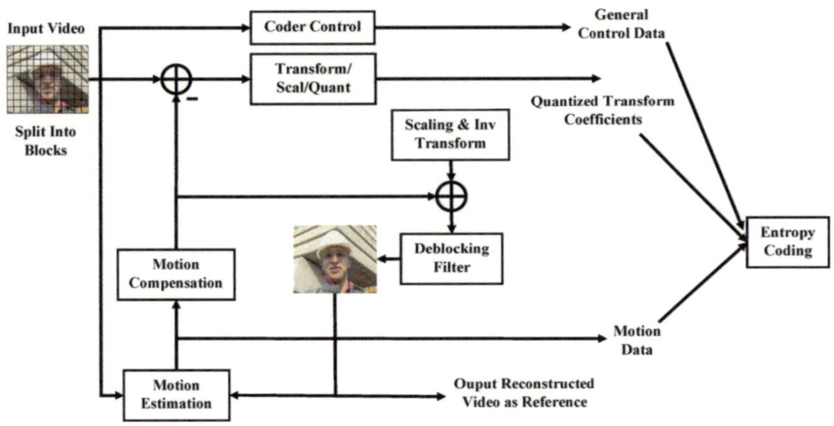

Figure 1.
Block diagram of the video compression process in the H.264/AVC standard [15].

H.264/AVC also uses intra-frame coding techniques to compress information within a single frame. These techniques involve dividing the frame into smaller blocks and using complex prediction models for each block. Additionally, the standard employs optimization techniques such as context-adaptive variable-length coding (CAVLC) and context-adaptive binary arithmetic coding (CABAC) to enhance compression efficiency. CABAC, in particular, is widely used in advanced profiles of H.264/AVC due to its more effective compression. **Figure 1** illustrates the block diagram of the video compression process in the H.264/AVC (advanced video coding) standard. In this standard, the input video signal is first divided into smaller blocks. The compression process begins with the application of encoder control and various transformations (transform/scaling/quantization) on these blocks. The transformed data is then sent to a scaling and inverse transformation unit for further optimization. An essential part of this process is motion compensation and motion estimation, used to reduce data size. The output of the reconstructed images is used as a reference, and the generated data is ultimately compressed through entropy coding for transmission or storage. Additionally, a deblocking filter is used to improve the final image quality. This diagram effectively shows the different stages and techniques used in the H.264/AVC standard [16].

The H.264/AVC standard has been successfully utilized in many applications, including digital television broadcasting, Blu-ray discs, video conferencing, online video streaming, and even in surveillance cameras and mobile devices. Its ability to maintain image quality with lower bitrates has made it the primary choice for many video streaming services, including YouTube and Netflix. Overall, H.264/AVC has played a crucial role in the development and advancement of multimedia technologies by providing a flexible and efficient compression framework and remains one of the most popular standards in video compression [17].

3.2.5 H.265/HEVC (introduced in 2013)

H.265/high efficiency video coding (HEVC) is an advanced video compression standard introduced in 2013 by ITU-T Video Coding Experts Group (VCEG) and ISO/IEC Moving Picture Experts Group (MPEG) as a successor to the H.264/AVC standard. The primary goal of HEVC was to enhance video compression efficiency, especially for high-resolution videos such as 4 and 8 K. HEVC managed to elevate the capabilities of H.264/AVC by further reducing bitrate without sacrificing image quality [18]. In fact, HEVC can reduce bitrate by up to 50% compared to H.264/AVC. Both AVC (Advanced Video Coding) and HEVC (High Efficiency Video Coding) are standards for video compression, but HEVC represents a significant advancement over AVC [19]. Known as H.265, HEVC offers major improvements in compression efficiency compared to AVC (H.264). HEVC can deliver the same image quality with half the bitrate, which reduces the need for bandwidth and storage space. These improvements are due to HEVC's more advanced techniques, such as larger block sizes (CTU), more precise motion prediction, and better coding at various scales (larger scales), leading to a significant enhancement in video compression [20].

One of the key innovations of HEVC is the use of larger and more flexible coding blocks. While H.264/AVC used fixed-size blocks (up to 16 x 16 pixels), HEVC employs an adaptive block structure known as coding tree unit (CTU), which can be up to 64 x 64 pixels. This increased block size allows HEVC to compress larger sections of an image more efficiently, especially in uniform and low-detail areas, significantly contributing to bitrate reduction. HEVC also utilizes more advanced motion prediction techniques. These standard employs more accurate motion vectors and new tools such as advanced motion vector prediction (AMVP) and Merge Mode, enhancing motion prediction accuracy. Additionally, HEVC uses more reference frames, which improves motion prediction quality and reduces bitrate. These capabilities enable HEVC to perform better in compressing videos with complex motion. Another notable feature of HEVC is its use of more efficient residual coding techniques. HEVC employs discrete cosine transform (DCT) and discrete sine transform (DST) as primary transform tools and, with adaptive quantization and more complex coding algorithms like context-adaptive binary arithmetic coding (CABAC), achieves further data reduction. These techniques enable HEVC to compress image data more effectively while maintaining significant image quality [21].

Intra-prediction modes are key components of video compression standards such as H.265/HEVC and H.266/VVC. These modes play a crucial role in optimizing the video compression process by predicting the values of internal pixels using the boundary information of neighboring blocks. This method reduces the need to transmit additional information, as in many cases, pixels of a block can be reconstructed using the predicted values. This process helps to reduce the data volume and consequently lower the bit rate while maintaining image quality. **Figure 2** relates to intra-prediction modes in video compression standards like H.265/HEVC or H.266/VVC. These modes are used to enhance video compression by predicting the pixels of a block through the use of boundary information from neighboring blocks. The figure highlights two basic modes: the planar mode (Mode 0), which creates a smooth gradient between horizontal and vertical edges, and the DC mode (Mode 1), which fills all pixels in the block with the average value of the boundary pixels. Additionally, horizontal modes (in the red area) predict pixel values by extending boundary information horizontally, while vertical modes (in the blue area) do so vertically [23]. Other modes, numbered 2–34, perform predictions at various angles between horizontal and vertical modes, increasing prediction accuracy and reducing bit rate. These angular modes are used to better adapt to different image structures, providing more efficient compression while preserving image quality.

One of the main challenges in using HEVC is its higher computational requirements. Due to the use of more advanced tools and increased algorithm complexity, HEVC necessitates more powerful hardware or longer encoding and decoding times. This initially posed limitations for widespread adoption of HEVC, but with

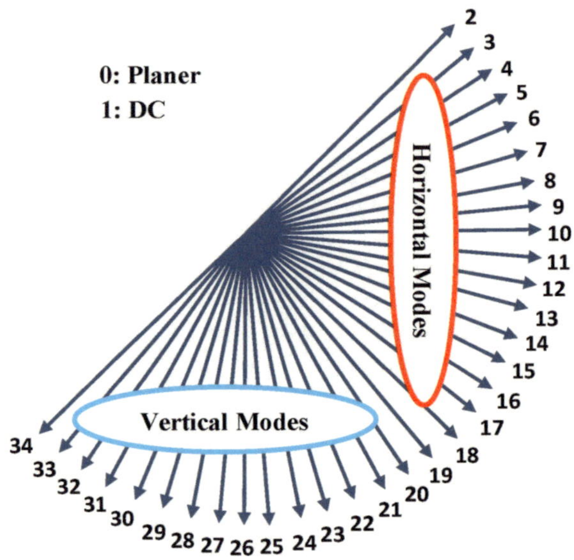

Figure 2.
Angular, planar, and DC modes in the HEVC standard [22].

advancements in technology and the availability of optimized processors and hardware devices, this issue has gradually diminished. **Figure 3** shows a block diagram of the video compression process in the H.265/high efficiency video coding (HEVC) standard. This standard, known as HEVC, was developed to improve the quality and efficiency of video compression compared to previous standards. In this process, the input video signal is first divided into coding units (CTUs), which serve as the

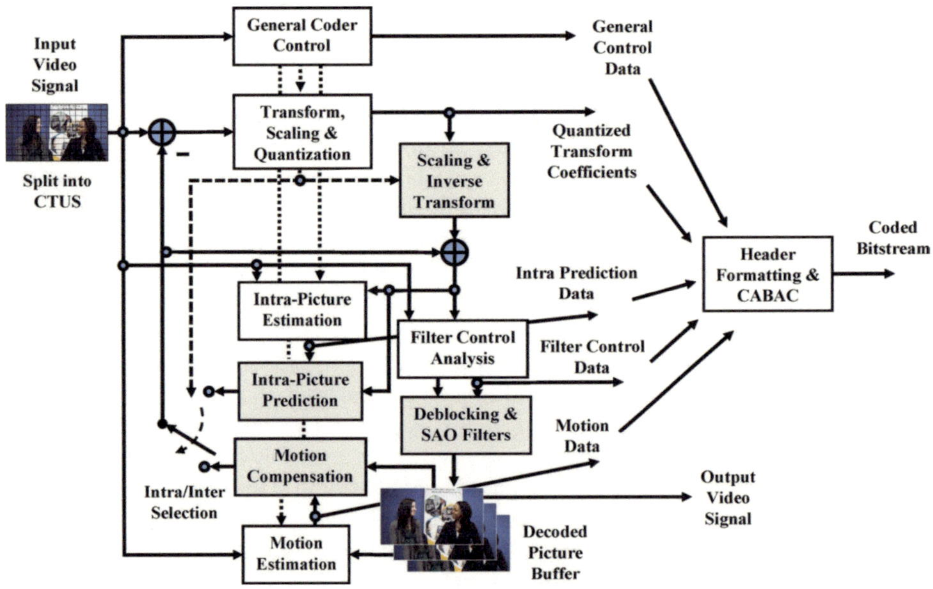

Figure 3.
Block diagram of the video compression process in the H.265/HEVC standard [24].

basic processing blocks and basis for compression. Then, information about luminance (brightness) and chrominance (color) is extracted from the image. Afterward, the signal is transformed into the frequency domain, scaled, and quantized to compress the data. In the prediction stage, parts of the image are estimated using data from the same image or previous frames. Motion compensation and motion estimation help reduce bitrate by identifying and estimating movement within frames. Additionally, various filters such as the deblocking filter and sample adaptive offset (SAO) filters are used to improve image quality. Finally, data is compressed using CABAC coding, and decoded images are stored in a buffer. The compressed bitstream is prepared for storage or transmission. This diagram effectively illustrates the advanced techniques and complex stages of video compression in the HEVC standard [25].

H.265/HEVC, as one of the primary video compression standards, is utilized in numerous modern applications, including 4 and 8 K television broadcasting, online video streaming, Ultra HD Blu-ray discs, and even in mobile devices. Due to the ever-increasing demand for high-quality video and limited bandwidth, HEVC has become a crucial standard in the multimedia industry. This standard plays a significant role in the development and advancement of video technologies by reducing bitrate while maintaining image quality, and it continues to be a leading option for high-quality video compression.

3.2.6 H.266/VVC (introduced in 2020)

Versatile video coding (VVC) is the latest video compression standard introduced in 2020 by the ITU-T Video Coding Experts Group (VCEG) and the ISO/IEC Moving Picture Experts Group (MPEG) as the successor to H.265/HEVC. VVC is designed to not only address current needs for compressing high-quality video such as 4 and 8 K but also to provide greater flexibility for various types of content, from virtual reality (VR) and 360-degree videos to high frame rate (HFR) content. This standard aims to reduce bitrate further compared to HEVC (by approximately 50%) without sacrificing image quality. A key feature of VVC is the use of a new coding structure called the coding tree unit (CTU), which operates similarly to HEVC but with greater flexibility and efficiency. VVC employs variable and optimized block sizes that can be up to 128 x 128 pixels, allowing for more efficient compression of different parts of the image. This block structure flexibility enables VVC to perform optimally under varying conditions and for diverse types of content [26].

Both high efficiency video coding (HEVC) and versatile video coding (VVC) are video compression standards that offer significant improvements over their predecessors. VVC, also known as H.266, is considerably more advanced than HEVC and can deliver image quality with a lower bitrate compared to HEVC. Key upgrades in VVC include the use of more advanced techniques such as even larger block partitions, improved motion prediction, and more complex compression algorithms that result in a substantial reduction in data volume and increased compression efficiency. VVC also enhances performance across different content conditions, including high definition and 3D video, providing more effective and flexible compression compared to HEVC. Significant advancements in VVC's motion prediction include the use of advanced techniques like multiple reference pictures (MRP) and adaptive motion vector prediction (AMVP), which offer greater accuracy in motion prediction and bitrate reduction. Additionally, VVC incorporates tools such as Optical Flow and more sophisticated motion prediction models that can better simulate and compress complex and nonlinear motion. Another innovation of VVC is in quantization and residual coding, employing more complex transforms like DCT-II, DCT-VIII, and DST-VII to compress image data with higher precision. The standard also utilizes advanced techniques for adaptive quantization and residual coding, which contribute to further data reduction while preserving high image quality [2].

VVC also enhances support for high dynamic range (HDR) and wide color gamut (WCG) content. This standard is capable of compressing videos with extended dynamic range and color gamut, contributing to the production of higher-quality video content. These features are particularly important for applications such as high-quality cinematic and television video broadcasting, which require accurate display of details and colors. In the realm of intra-frame encoding, VVC employs optimized methods like matrix intra prediction (MIP) and intra sub partitioning (ISP), which offer higher precision in compressing intra-frame information. These tools help VVC achieve better performance in compressing static images and fixed segments of videos. Additionally, VVC utilizes new techniques for encoding keyframes that can further reduce bitrate and enhance compression efficiency. VVC also includes optimizations for parallel processing and the use of multiple processing cores, which enable faster and more efficient video encoding and decoding. This feature is particularly significant for applications that require rapid processing of large video files, such as live video streaming or high-quality video editing. By leveraging parallel processing, VVC can better utilize the processing power of devices and reduce processing time [27].

Figure 4 depicts the block diagram of the video compression process in the H.266/ versatile video coding (VVC) standard, illustrating the various stages through which a video signal undergoes compression. In this process, the input video signal is first divided into coding tree units (CTUs). Next, information related to luminance and chrominance is extracted. The signal is then transformed from the temporal domain to the frequency domain, and the transformed data is scaled and quantized. During

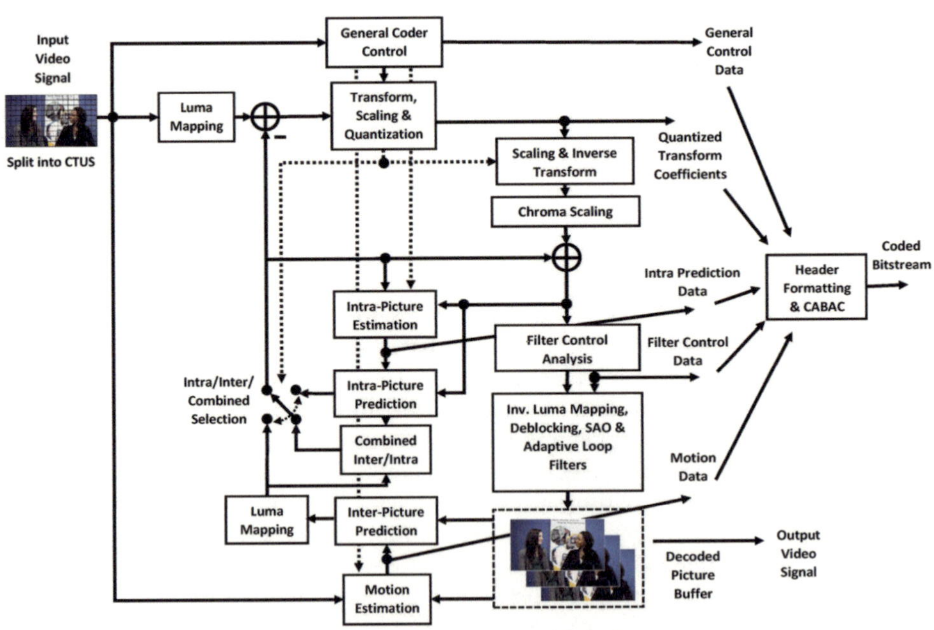

Figure 4.
Block diagram of the video compression process in the H.266/VVC standard [28].

the prediction phase, parts of the image are estimated using data from the same image or previous frames. Various filters are then applied to enhance image quality. Finally, the data is compressed using encoding methods such as CABAC and the decoded images are stored in a buffer. The bitstream of the encoded data is prepared as the final output of the compression process, ready for transmission or storage. This diagram effectively demonstrates the complexities and various stages of the VVC standard for achieving high-quality and efficient video compression.

Due to its advanced capabilities, VVC is utilized in various applications, including television broadcasting, online video streaming, video conferencing, virtual reality (VR) videos, and even video games. This standard plays a crucial role in reducing data transfer costs and improving the user experience by offering higher quality and requiring less bandwidth. Overall, VVC is expected to play a key role in the future of video technology by providing an advanced and flexible video compression framework. Each of these standards, with their innovations, has contributed to shaping the future of video compression and plays a vital role in advancing multimedia technology by reducing network and storage resource needs.

4. Comparison of video compression algorithms

4.1 Evaluation criteria: Image quality, computational complexity, storage requirements, bit rate

When evaluating and comparing video compression algorithms, four primary criteria are considered:

Image quality: Image quality refers to the extent to which video details are preserved after compression. This criterion is particularly important as it reflects the final visual experience of the user. Various tools, such as peak signal-to-noise ratio (PSNR) and structural similarity index (SSIM), are used to measure image quality after compression. Each compression algorithm strives to balance data reduction with image quality preservation [29].

Computational complexity: Computational complexity refers to the amount of processing resources required to execute the compression algorithm. More complex algorithms might provide better image quality but require more processing resources. This criterion is crucial for applications that need fast or real-time compression, as computational resources may be limited [30].

Storage requirements: This criterion pertains to the volume of compressed data and the need for storage space. Different algorithms produce varying amounts of data depending on their compression methods. The choice of algorithm may vary based on storage needs and available storage space [31].

Bit rate: Bit rate is a measure of the amount of data transmitted per second and is directly related to image quality and bandwidth requirements. Different algorithms may produce different bit rates depending on the compression techniques used. Optimizing bit rate without compromising image quality is one of the primary goals in video compression [32].

4.2 Comparison of algorithm performance under similar conditions

In this section, the performance of video compression algorithms is compared under similar conditions in terms of image quality, computational complexity, storage requirements, and bit rate. This comparison includes examining how algorithms perform in various scenarios, including high- and low-resolution videos, different frame rates, and diverse content types (such as fast-moving scenes or static scenes). Detailed comparisons using empirical data and standard tests are conducted to determine which algorithm performs best under different conditions. This analysis helps in understanding the advantages and limitations of each algorithm [33].

4.3 Examination of different applications and algorithm suitability

In this section, video compression algorithms are reviewed for their suitability for various applications. Some algorithms may be more suitable for applications like online video streaming, which require low bit rates and acceptable image quality. Other algorithms might be more appropriate for high-quality video storage or environments with limited bandwidth. This section explores different applications, including live streaming, video conferencing, cinematic video archiving, educational videos, and more, and introduces the algorithms best suited for each application [34].

5. Optimization of video compression

5.1 Utilization of artificial intelligence and deep learning in compression

The application of artificial intelligence (AI) and deep learning in video compression has emerged as one of the most advanced approaches in recent years. These techniques analyze and learn complex patterns in video data to achieve optimizations in the compression process that traditional methods cannot. Deep learning models can automatically identify critical image components and precisely remove unnecessary sections, thus minimizing data size while preserving image quality. These techniques also help improve the quality of compressed images, reduce bit rates, and enhance compression speed [35].

5.2 Adaptive and dynamic coding techniques

Adaptive and dynamic coding techniques are specifically designed to adjust compression parameters based on video content changes and transmission conditions. Instead of using fixed parameters throughout the video, these methods dynamically alter parameters like bit rate, resolution, and intra- and inter-coding based on the need. These techniques are particularly useful in environments with limited bandwidth or constantly changing video content. For instance, in scenes with high motion, the bit rate increases, while in static scenes, it decreases, optimizing bandwidth usage and improving image quality [36].

5.3 Content-based compression techniques

Content-based compression refers to adaptive methods that adjust compression settings and algorithms according to the type of video content. For example, videos with simple content and minimal movement can use lossless compression techniques, whereas videos with complex content and rapid motion may use methods that more significantly reduce data size. This approach directly enhances compression efficiency and improves image quality relative to the content type [37].

5.4 Role of GPUs and specialized hardware in compression optimization

Graphics processing units (GPUs) and specialized hardware play a crucial role in optimizing the video compression process. GPUs are designed for parallel processing and can handle vast amounts of video data at high speeds. Utilizing GPUs in video compression, especially for applications requiring simultaneous processing of multiple video frames, increases efficiency and reduces processing time. Additionally, specialized hardware such as application-specific integrated circuits (ASICs) and field-programmable gate arrays (FPGAs) is designed for high-performance compression algorithms. These hardware solutions can be specifically optimized for particular compression needs and are highly effective in real-time processing applications [38].

5.5 Major applications of video compression

Online video streaming is one of the most widespread applications of video compression, where videos are transmitted either live or on-demand over the Internet. Compression plays a crucial role in reducing both bandwidth and storage requirements, allowing high-quality video playback over networks with limited capacity. Algorithms such as H.264/AVC, H.265/HEVC, and VVC are designed to deliver high-quality images at low bit rates, ensuring a smooth and uninterrupted viewing experience for users, even on slower connections. In video conferencing, maintaining both image quality and minimizing latency is essential. Video compression reduces the amount of data that needs to be transmitted, which helps improve the overall connection quality and lowers latency [39]. Compression algorithms are particularly important in ensuring that live, synchronous communications remain clear and uninterrupted, whether for business meetings or educational purposes. Techniques such as dynamic coding and adaptive compression further enhance performance by adjusting to changing network conditions in real time. For surveillance and security systems, video compression is vital to manage and store large volumes of video data. By reducing data size, compression allows for long-term storage without significantly sacrificing the quality required for tasks such as identification and analysis. This is particularly important for CCTV cameras and other surveillance systems, which must record and store vast amounts of footage while ensuring acceptable image quality for security purposes [40].

In the context of video games and virtual reality (VR), video compression is essential for delivering high-quality visuals while minimizing the demands on bandwidth and processing power. VR, in particular, relies on compression techniques to stream and render high-quality 3D videos in real-time. Advanced compression methods help manage the large data volumes and complex interactions found in modern gaming and VR environments, improving the user experience and reducing delays in processing and transmission. Large-scale video data storage, such as in data centers or video archives, also relies on video compression to manage vast amounts of data efficiently. By reducing storage space requirements, compression makes it possible to store large volumes of video while maintaining image quality over extended periods. This helps improve the overall efficiency of storage systems, making it easier to organize and preserve video data under various storage conditions [41].

6. Challenges and future of video compression

6.1 Technical challenges (quality, bit rate, latency)

Maintaining image quality after compression is one of the primary challenges, as increasing compression to reduce data size may degrade image quality, causing a loss of details and colors. Compression algorithms must balance data reduction with preserving image quality. Bit rate directly impacts both the quality and size of compressed data; while a higher bit rate can enhance image quality, it also requires more bandwidth and storage space, so effective algorithms must manage bit rate optimally. Additionally, latency in video compression is crucial for applications like live streaming and video conferencing, where minimizing processing and transmission delays is essential for an enhanced user experience [42].

6.2 Compatibility with new formats and emerging standards

With the emergence of new formats and standards, such as H.266/VVC and AV1, ensuring compatibility of existing algorithms with these standards becomes a significant challenge. These new standards continuously evolve and offer improvements in compression. Algorithms must support these standards while also being compatible with existing formats to be effectively used across diverse systems and environments [2].

6.3 The future of compression with 8 K and beyond

As video resolution and quality advance to 8 K and beyond, new challenges for video compression arise. Compressing 8 K video requires more advanced algorithms capable of managing very high data volumes while preserving extremely high image quality. This necessitates new technologies and further optimizations in compression algorithms to meet the increasing demands for high-resolution content [43].

6.4 Impact of emerging technologies like 5G and 6G on video compression

Emerging technologies such as 5G and 6G will have a significant impact on video compression. These technologies offer higher speeds and lower latency, leading to substantial improvements in data transmission. Video compression can leverage these technologies to enhance streaming and virtual reality experiences and reduce bandwidth requirements. Additionally, these technologies will aid in developing and optimizing compression algorithms for use in high-speed, high-capacity networks [44].

7. Conclusion

7.1 Summary of key points

In this chapter, various aspects of video compression were examined and analyzed. The video compression process includes key stages such as data analysis, redundancy reduction, and final encoding, each playing a crucial role in reducing data volume and optimizing video storage and transmission. Various coding techniques, including intra and inter-coding, motion prediction, and quantization, were highlighted for their importance in effective video compression. Additionally, a comprehensive comparison of different compression algorithms was presented, focusing on criteria such as image quality, computational complexity, storage requirements, and bit rate. Modern optimization techniques, including the use of artificial intelligence and deep learning, adaptive and dynamic coding, content-based compression, and the role of GPUs and specialized hardware, were discussed. The diverse applications of video compression, including online video streaming, video conferencing, surveillance and security systems, video games and virtual reality, and large-scale video data storage, underscore the importance of this technology across various domains.

7.2 Future trends in video compression

The future of video compression will be influenced by technological advancements and evolving user needs. With the emergence of higher resolutions such as 8 K and ongoing improvements in compression standards, there will be an increased demand for more efficient and optimized compression algorithms. Additionally, emerging technologies like 5G and 6G will provide significant improvements in data transmission, enabling high-quality video experiences with minimal latency. Research and innovations in artificial intelligence and deep learning for enhancing the video compression process are progressing, and these techniques are expected to play a vital role in optimizing image quality, reducing bit rates, and improving compression efficiency. Overall, future trends in video compression will focus on improving quality, reducing data volume, and ensuring compatibility with new technologies and emerging standards.

Author details

Yaghoub Saberi*, Mohammadreza Forghani and Sharifeh S. Mirkhalaf
Department of Computer Engineering, Najafabad Branch, Islamic Azad University, Najafabad, Iran

*Address all correspondence to: y.saberi@sco.iaun.ac.ir

References

[1] Lee DY et al. A subjective and objective study of space-time subsampled video quality. IEEE Transactions on Image Processing. 2022;**31**:934-948. DOI: 10.1109/tip.2021.3137658

[2] Choi K. A study on fast and low-complexity algorithms for versatile video coding. Sensors (Basel). 2022;**22**(22):8990. DOI: 10.3390/s22228990

[3] Luo Z, Chai B, Wang Z, Hu M, Wu D. Masked360: Enabling robust 360-degree video streaming with ultra low bandwidth consumption. IEEE Transactions on Visualization and Computer Graphics. 2023:2690-2699. DOI: 10.1109/tvcg.2023.3247076

[4] Wu C, He G, Lai X, Li Y. MPCNet: Compressed multi-view video restoration via motion-parallax complementation network. Neural Networks. 2023;**167**:601-614. DOI: 10.1016/j.neunet.2023.08.037

[5] Bai Y, Liu X, Wang K, Ji X, Wu X, Gao W. Deep Lossy plus residual coding for lossless and near-lossless image compression. IEEE Transactions on Pattern Analysis and Machine Intelligence. 2024;**46**(5):3577-3594. DOI: 10.1109/tpami.2023.3348486

[6] Dinesh C, Cheung G, Bajic IV. Point cloud video super-resolution via partial point coupling and graph smoothness. IEEE Transactions on Image Processing. 2022;**31**:4117-4132. DOI: 10.1109/tip.2022.3166644

[7] Filicori F et al. SAGES video acquisition framework-analysis of available OR recording technologies by the SAGES AI task force. Surgical Endoscopy. 2023;**37**(6):4321-4327. DOI: 10.1007/s00464-022-09825-3

[8] Liang Z, Liu J, Dasari M, Wang F. Fumos: Neural compression and progressive refinement for continuous point cloud video streaming. IEEE Transactions on Visualization and Computer Graphics. 2024;**30**(5):2849-2859. DOI: 10.1109/tvcg.2024.3372096

[9] Parikh SS, Ruiz D, Kalva H, Fernandez-Escribano G, Adzic V. High bit-depth medical image compression with HEVC. IEEE Journal of Biomedical and Health Informatics. 2018;**22**(2):552-560. DOI: 10.1109/jbhi.2017.2660482

[10] Ouyang M, Chen Z. JPEG quantized coefficient recovery via DCT domain spatial-frequential transformer. IEEE Transactions on Image Processing. 2024;**33**:3385-3398. DOI: 10.1109/tip.2024.3403054

[11] Ni CT, Huang YC, Chen PY. A hardware-friendly and high-efficiency H.265/HEVC encoder for visual sensor networks. Sensors (Basel). 2023;**23**(5):2625. DOI: 10.3390/s23052625

[12] Mico-Enguidanos F, Salcedo-Navarro A, Garcia-Pineda M, Gutierrez-Aguado J. Features and quality metrics datasets for video coding in DASH. Scientific Data. 2024;**11**(1):696. DOI: 10.1038/s41597-024-03507-6

[13] Belyaev E. An efficient compressive sensed video codec with inter-frame decoding and low-complexity intra-frame encoding. Sensors (Basel). 2023;**23**(3):1368. DOI: 10.3390/s23031368

[14] Lu G, Zhang X, Ouyang W, Chen L, Gao Z, Xu D. An end-to-end learning framework for video compression. IEEE Transactions on Pattern Analysis and Machine Intelligence.

2021;**43**(10):3292-3308. DOI: 10.1109/tpami.2020.2988453

[15] Dalal M, Juneja M. H. 264/AVC video steganography techniques: An overview. International Journal of Computational Science and Engineering. 2018;**6**(5):297-303

[16] Wang Z, Wang S, Zhang X, Wang S, Ma S. Three-zone segmentation based motion compensation for video compression. IEEE Transactions on Image Processing. 2019:5091-5104. DOI: 10.1109/tip.2019.2910382

[17] Bampis CG, Zhi L, Moorthy AK, Katsavounidis I, Aaron A, Bovik AC. Study of temporal effects on subjective video quality of experience. IEEE Transactions on Image Processing. 2017;**26**(11):5217-5231. DOI: 10.1109/tip.2017.2729891

[18] Saberi Y, Ramezanpour M, Fekri-Ershad S, Barekatain B. CBIR-ACHS: Compressed domain content-based image retrieval through auto-correloblock in HEVC standard. In: Multimedia Tools and Applications. Cham, Switzerland: Springer; 2024. pp. 1-17

[19] Ramezanpour M, Zargari F. Fast CU size and prediction mode decision method for HEVC encoder based on spatial features. Signal, Image and Video Processing. 2016;**10**(7):1233-1240

[20] Fini MR, Zargari Asl F. A fast intra mode decision method based on reduction of the number of modes in HEVC standard. In: 7'th International Symposium on Telecommunications (IST'2014). Piscataway, NJ, USA: IEEE; 2014. pp. 839-843

[21] Najafabadi N, Ramezanpour M. Mass center direction-based decision method for intraprediction in HEVC standard. Journal of Real-Time Image Processing. 2020;**17**(5):1153-1168

[22] Saberi Y, Ramezanpour M, Khorsand R. An efficient data hiding method using the intra prediction modes in HEVC. Multimedia Tools and Applications. 2020;**79**(43):33279-33302

[23] Ramezanpour M, Zargari F. Fast HEVC I-frame coding based on strength of dominant direction of CUs. Journal of Real-Time Image Processing. 2016;**12**(2):397-406

[24] Subbarayappa S, Rao K. Overview and extensions of the high efficiency video coding (HEVC) and beyond (versatile video coding). International Journal of Emerging Technology and Advanced Engineering. 2019;**9**(12):70-97

[25] Kaczynski M, Piotrowski Z, Pietrow D. High-quality video watermarking based on deep neural networks for video with HEVC compression. Sensors (Basel). 2022;**22**(19):7552. DOI: 10.3390/s22197552

[26] Feng A, Liu K, Liu D, Li L, Wu F. Partition map prediction for fast block partitioning in VVC intra-frame coding. IEEE Transactions on Image Processing. 2023;**32**:2237-2251. DOI: 10.1109/tip.2023.3266165

[27] Luo D, Xiong S, Ren C, Sheriff RE, He X. Fusion-based versatile video coding intra prediction algorithm with template matching and linear prediction. Sensors (Basel). 2022;**22**(16):5977. DOI: 10.3390/s22165977

[28] Bross B et al. Overview of the versatile video coding (VVC) standard and its applications. IEEE Transactions on Circuits and Systems for Video Technology. 2021;**31**(10):3736-3764

[29] Mahdaoui AE, Ouahabi A, Moulay MS. Image denoising using a compressive sensing approach based on regularization constraints. Sensors

(Basel). 2022;**22**(6):2199. DOI: 10.3390/s22062199

[30] Yang Y et al. Multi-criterion sampling matting algorithm via Gaussian process. Biomimetics (Basel). 2023;**8**(3):10. DOI: 10.3390/biomimetics8030301

[31] Purica A, Boyadjis B, Pesquet-Popescu B, Dufaux F, Bergeron C. A convex optimization framework for video quality and resolution enhancement from multiple descriptions. IEEE Transactions on Image Processing. 2019;**28**(4):1661-1674. DOI: 10.1109/tip.2018.2880567

[32] Schwartz C, Sander I, Bruhn F, Persson M, Ekblad J, Fuglesang C. Satellite image compression guided by regions of interest. Sensors (Basel). 2023;**23**(2):730. DOI: 10.3390/s23020730

[33] Sheng L, Ngan KN, Lim CL, Li S. Online temporally consistent indoor depth video enhancement via static structure. IEEE Transactions on Image Processing. 2015;**24**(7):2197-2211. DOI: 10.1109/tip.2015.2416658

[34] Liu Z, Pan X, Li Y, Chen Z. A game theory based CTU-level bit allocation scheme for HEVC region of interest coding. IEEE Transactions on Image Processing. 2021;**30**:794-805. DOI: 10.1109/tip.2020.3038515

[35] Seng JKP, Ang KL-M, Peter E, Mmonyi A. Artificial intelligence (AI) and machine learning for multimedia and edge information processing. Electronics. 2022;**11**(14):2239

[36] Ashok Kumar PM, Arun Raj LN, Jyothi B, Soliman NF, Bajaj M, El-Shafai W. A novel dynamic bit rate analysis technique for adaptive video streaming over HTTP support. Sensors (Basel). 2022;**22**(23):9307. DOI: 10.3390/s22239307

[37] Lee Y, Hirakawa K. Lossless white balance for improved lossless CFA image and video compression. IEEE Transactions on Image Processing. 2022;**31**:3309-3321. DOI: 10.1109/tip.2022.3169687

[38] Satheesh Kumar N, Arun C. A novel video compression model based on GPU virtualization with CUDA platform using bi-directional RNN. International Journal of Information Technology. 2024;**16**(1):457-463

[39] Zhang Z et al. A decade review of video compressive sensing: A roadmap to practical applications. In: Engineering. Amsterdam, Netherlands: Elsevier; 2024

[40] Hoang TM, Zhou J. Recent trending on learning based video compression: A survey. Cognitive Robotics. 2021;**1**:145-158

[41] Jeong J, Jang D, Son J, Ryu ES. 3DoF+ 360 video location-based asymmetric down-sampling for view synthesis to immersive VR video streaming. Sensors (Basel). 2018;**18**(9):3148. DOI: 10.3390/s18093148

[42] Sinno Z, Bovik AC. Large-scale study of perceptual video quality. IEEE Transactions on Image Processing. 2018:612-627. DOI: 10.1109/tip.2018.2869673

[43] Yamashita H, Kobayashi E. Mechanism and design of a novel 8K ultra-high-definition video microscope for microsurgery. Heliyon. 2021;**7**(2):e06244. DOI: 10.1016/j.heliyon.2021.e06244

[44] Puspitasari AA, An TT, Alsharif MH, Lee BM. Emerging technologies for 6G communication networks: Machine learning approaches. Sensors (Basel). 2023;**23**(18):7709. DOI: 10.3390/s23187709